Pigging Out in Savannah

Pigging Out in Savannah

◆

A Restaurant Guide to Savannah

Cathy Swift
Van Robbins
John Miltiades

iUniverse, Inc.
New York Lincoln Shanghai

Pigging Out in Savannah
A Restaurant Guide to Savannah

Copyright © 2008 by 3 Little Piggies, Inc.

All rights reserved. No part of this book may be used or reproduced by any means, graphic, electronic, or mechanical, including photocopying, recording, taping or by any information storage retrieval system without the written permission of the publisher except in the case of brief quotations embodied in critical articles and reviews.

iUniverse books may be ordered through booksellers or by contacting:

iUniverse
2021 Pine Lake Road, Suite 100
Lincoln, NE 68512
www.iuniverse.com
1-800-Authors (1-800-288-4677)

Because of the dynamic nature of the Internet, any Web addresses or links contained in this book may have changed since publication and may no longer be valid.

The views expressed in this work are solely those of the author and do not necessarily reflect the views of the publisher, and the publisher hereby disclaims any responsibility for them.

ISBN: 978-0-595-48632-8 (pbk)
ISBN: 978-0-595-60726-6 (ebk)

Printed in the United States of America

Contents

Bon Appetit ix
The Three Little Piggies xi
Savannah's Historic Area 1
    45 Bistro 1
    514 West 2
    700 Drayton 3
    1790 Restaurant 4
    Alligator Soul 5
    Aqua Star (Westin Resort) 6
    A Vida Restaurant & Wine Bar 7
    B. Matthews 8
    Belford's 9
    Boar's Head Grill and Tavern 10
    Carlito's 11
    Cha Bella Grill & Patio Bar 12
    Chart House 13
    Clary's 14
    Cobblestone Conch House 15
    Cotton Exchange Tavern 16
    Courtyard Café 17
    Firefly Café 18
    Garibaldi's 19
    Huey's on the River 20
    Il Pasticcio 21
    Isaac's at 9 Drayton 22

Jazz'd	23
Lady and Sons	24
Local 11 Ten	25
Magnolia Restaurant	27
Mrs. Wilkes Dining Room	28
Olde Pink House	29
Olympia Café	30
Pirates' House	31
River House Seafood	32
Sapphire Grill	33
Season's Asian Bistro	34
Shrimp Factory	35
Skyler's	36
Soho South Café	37
Sushi Zen	38
Tapas	39
Vic's on the River	40
Window's Restaurant	41

Savannah Originals Not to be Missed—Located Outside the Historic Area 42

Elizabeth's on 37th	42
Johnny Harris	43

Which Way to Tybee? 45

Crab Shack	45
Hunter House	46
The Breakfast Club	47
Uncle Bubba's	48

Savannah's Bar Food 50

AJ's Dockside Restaurant	50
B & D Burgers	50
Bernie's	51
Bonna Bella Yacht Club	52

Churchill's Restaurant & Tavern 52
Creekside Grill 53
Creole Red 54
Crystal Beer Parlor 54
Jen's and Friends 55
Kevin Barry's Irish Pub 55
Loco's Deli and Pub 56
Lulu's Chocolate Bar 56
McDonough's 57
Mellow Mushroom 58
Molly MacPherson's Scottish Pub & Grill 58
Moon River Brewing Company 59
One-Eyed Lizzy's 59
Oyster Bar 60
Six Pence Pub 60
Spanky's 61
Tubby's Tank House 62
Vinnie Van Go Go 62
Wild Wing Café 63

Glossary of Savannah Food Terms 65
Parking in Savannah 69

Bon Appetit

Eating our way through Savannah was a daunting task, but we figured someone needed to do it and who was better equipped than The 3 Little Piggies! We gained a collective 40 pounds, enjoyed many laughs, had an occasional Rolaid or two, maxed out our credit cards, and wondered whether we qualified for AA (considering all the wonderful wines, martinis and libations that we just had to have with our dinners!) We had so much fun that we decided this guide would need updated on an annual basis.

Seriously, one fact that emerged during our "research" was that Savannah is a force to be reckoned with in the war of gastronomic dominance. One can go to New York (Snobby), Las Vegas (High-Flying), Atlanta (Southern Wannabe), or New Orleans (Recovering), but here in Savannah, along with the fine food, are romance, history, mystery, intrigue, and quirkiness. How much better can it get?

We love our city, and many do not want to see it change. Savannians see change as evil, i.e., a force that will negatively affect our slow way of life, our small town spirit, or the "hidden" secrets which have been prolifically recorded (*Midnight in the Garden of Good and Evil, Delirium of the Brave, Savannah Blues*). However, when it comes to food and drink, we are the gold medal winners of progress. We are known to celebrate everything from the mundane to the catastrophic, as evidenced by the elaborate parties taking place when a possible hurricane approaches. Don't worry though, we have the evacuation down pat; we just know how to put some dazzle and style in to make the process more fun!

The first question asked of a stranger in Charleston would be "Who are your people?" In Atlanta it is "Where are you employed?" Here in Savannah with true gentility, the question first asked is "What can I get you to drink?" For you see, there are no strangers in Savannah, only guests who we are all excited about getting to know better. There is no better way of doing this than by breaking bread, sharing a plate and raising a glass together. Hopefully, this book will make you feel at home in our fine city, and feel that you are our friends, and not just visitors.

The Three Little Piggies

Cat (Cathy Swift), as a Professor of Marketing at Georgia Southern University, anonymously wrote the column, "Let's Do Lunch," for the *Savannah Business Journal*. Unlike this book, that column focused on restaurant reviews from a business lunch perspective. This Brick Pig now resides in Fairview, TX and works for MERLOT (the organization: www.merlot.org not the wine!) as Director of Academic Partner Services.

Van (Van Robbins) got her start from Savannah native, Juliette Gordon Low, the founder of the Girl Scouts. Their mothers were best friends, so it was only natural that Van and Juliette hung out together. Juliette founded the Girl Scouts of the USA, of which Van was an active member. In fact, this Straw Pig was the originator of the Cooking Badge, and to this day considers that her finest achievement.

Him (John Miltiades) is a direct descendant of General James Oglethorpe and is considered a scholar, captain of tall ships, and builder of large buildings. He holds world records in fishing, skinny dipping, and sport crabbing. When he was offered the opportunity to become a pig, he jumped. While he says he does not know which pig is brick or straw, we all kind of know in our hearts who the MudPig is.

The 3 Little Piggies share their views of some of the best opportunities to "pig out" in Savannah. The restaurants appear in alphabetical order. The opinions are those of the authors only. We visited the restaurants anonymously and did not receive any special favors from any of the locations. Our only compensation was bigger waistlines, credit card debt, and satisfaction knowing we sampled the best that Savannah has to offer.

Savannah's Historic Area

45 Bistro

123 E. Broughton Street
912-234-3111

45 Bistro is located in the Marshall House Inn, a historic Inn that opened in 1851. It was fully restored and renovated in 1999 and is known as Savannah's Oldest Inn. The restaurant is located off the lobby and is quaint, intimate, and definitely romantic!

45 Bistro offers some of the finest cuisine in Savannah. An excellent starter is the Sautéed Veal Sweetbreads with sweet potato shoestrings and pomegranate e glace mole. It is delicious, and the sweetbreads are an absolute taste treat! 45 Bistro offers Wood-Fired Pizzas—go for the pizza topped with local shrimp, pesto, red onion, olives and cherve (are we in Tuscany?!).

The salads deserve special mention. A favorite is the Grilled Hearts of Romaine served with traditional Caesar dressing, but the innovative offering is the Satay of Lamb Tenderloin over romaine lettuce with kalamata olives, roasted red peppers, feta cheese, cucumber, tomato, and lemon parsley vinaigrette.

The Veal Osso Bucco is the best we have ever eaten. The veal is fork tender, flavorful, and served over mushroom saffron risotto. If steak is what you want, try the Seared Filet Mignon, served au poivere, with Gorgonzola gratinee and pomme frites, fresh arugula and a tarragon roasted garlic aioli. An incredibly delicious southern specialty is the Grilled Bourbon Split Double Pork Chop stuffed with braised collard greens, wild mushroom dressing, and topped with caramelized Vidalia onion cognac cream.

Our server was excellent and attentive to every need. The wine list is extensive and 'forced' us to sample more wine than intended!!

As Savannah is so historic, we are lucky to have such a gastronomic icon as 45 Bistro to grace our dining history book!

Cat: I love the Grilled Salad. Since lettuce is mostly water, I think I could make this and it wouldn't burn!
Van: My favorite is the Sweetbreads!
Him: I ordered that—where was the bread? And it wasn't sweet either!

514 West

514 W. Martin Luther King Boulevard
912-236-7409

514 West is a delightful restaurant located downtown right on the cusp of the historic district. The restaurant derives its name from its address at 514 West Martin Luther King Boulevard. 514 West is in a building which has been tastefully refurbished, the interior is brick and wood, and is accented by black and white photographs of jazz musicians.

The delicious Cheese-Garlic Biscuits start your appetite humming. You'll be tempted to eat several of them, but be sure to save room for other appetizers including Southern' Blue's' Crab Cakes, Homemade Chicken Pate, and White Bean Soup with Chorizo Sausage.

The restaurant offers a variety of dishes including seafood, duck, lamb, steak and pasta. The Muscovy Duck Breast is delicious, as is the Black Angus Fillet Rossini. For those who choose seafood or fish, we recommend King Crab (in season), Canadian King Salmon or the Fresh Copper River Salmon.

The restaurant offers full bar with a wide selection of domestic and imported beer and wine as well as other alcoholic drinks. Plan on having drinks outside in the courtyard, so you can enjoy the ambiance of Savannah.

This masterpiece is a crescendo to a perfect day in Savannah!

Him: Cool! 5 = 1 + 4!!!
Van: Are you smarter than a fifth grader?

Cat: And to think.... I'm a college professor!

700 Drayton
700 Drayton Street
912-341-0700

One of the biggest events of Savannah was the opening of The Mansion on Forsyth Park, an 1888 Savannah mansion that transitioned from an elegant funeral parlor to an elegant, eclectic, eccentric, elaborate establishment for overnight stays and fine dining.

700 Drayton is THE destination restaurant of Savannah, and features 16 foot ceilings, 6 fireplaces, a massive wine cellar, and a stunning Bosendorfer piano. This is in addition to the vintage hat collection, vintage art, and very unique chandeliers!

Casimir's Lounge is the perfect start to have a 'spirit' and to ward away 'the spirits'! The wine list is extensive, as are the martini creations. After your aperitif, get ready for gastronomic levitation!!

THE VIEWING
There are many showings for this course, a favorite being the Blue Crab Cake and Tasso Gumbo served over a corn pancake, Bourbon Buttered Leeks and Black Eyed Pea Cakes. Another personal favorite is the 700 Tuna Tartar which is yellow fin tuna, dried dates, almond, lemon confit, harissa, fine herbs, cumin, crispy egg roll chips, cilantro lime vinaigrette and a warm shiitake salad (if you want the kitchen sink, it is an added price!).

The EVENT
GLORY, GLORY, GLORY!!! Pan Roasted Gulf Coast Grouper with Georgia shrimp fricassee, butter poached asparagus, country ham, herbed grit cake, and spiced cioppino broth is divine, as is Pan Roasted Chilean Sea Bass with saffron shellfish stew, heirloom tomato relish, crawfish herb risotto, grilled corn bread and lemon butter. If fowl is to your liking, the Stuffed Breast of Chicken with garlic mustard greens, sweet corn succotash, and warm apple wood bacon vinaigrette and creamy polenta will be sure to have you singing from the rafters!

VISITATION

Relax and enjoy the White Chocolate Banana Bread Pudding served with vanilla bean ice cream, or Molten Chocolate Cake, or Grand Marnier Chocolate Truffle Mousse Cake, or Warm Apple Crisp, or.... I think I've just died and gone to heaven!

Cat: I can't wait to get to Heaven if the food is like this!
Van: Can we write a "Food in Heaven Review"?
Him: Can I go to Heaven too??!!!

1790 Restaurant

307 E. President Street
912-236-7122

The 17Hundred90 Restaurant is located in the basement of the city's oldest Inn at 307 E. President Street. The Inn and restaurant are comprised of 2 homes that were built in the 1790's and the brick walls and the stone floors are original. Of course, the requisite ghost is in attendance, but more about that later!

Start with the Crab Cakes (local back-fin crab with a Cajun remoulade) and the House Cured Gravlox (served with dill, capers and red onion),as both are quite tasty. Also sample the 1790 Specialty Salad, mixed greens, golden raisins, walnuts, Stilton cheese, dressed with raspberry vinaigrette dressing.

For entrees we recommend Pecan Encrusted Grouper, the Stuffed Shrimp (stuffed with scallops and crabmeat), the Rack of Lamb (with garlic and rosemary) and the Half Roasted Duckling (served with port wine and lingonberry sauce) and accompanied by creamed corn and rice.

Be sure to save room for dessert. The 17Hundred90 Specialty Bread Pudding is delicious as it is soaked in bourbon sauce. Equally delicious is the Chocolate Bombe, flour-less chocolate torte with Raspberry sauce. If you haven't tasted it anywhere else, the Savannah Mud Pie is also a yummy choice.

Okay, so back to the ghost. It is alleged that a young woman threw herself from a 3rd floor window to the brick courtyard below, causing her death, after watching her married seaman lover leave on a ship. It's rumored that she is still waiting his return, and especially haunts room 204. We guess that this is the true definition of unrequited love!!!!

Van: I'll bet he didn't return because he did not ask for directions!
Him: I've had many a drink with the ghost!
Cat: Maybe "1790 Bottles of Beer on the wall?"

Alligator Soul
114 Barnard Street
912-232-7899

Alligator Soul is a small, intimate restaurant with beautiful brick walls, a warm inviting fireplace, and intimate cozy tables. It is known for artistic food, creations based on the exotic and unique. The menu is reminiscent of the plantation days—when wild game was the mainstay of daily fare. The appetizers are varied and include cheese courses, their signature specialty gumbos, and lamb skewers on a Greek Salad with chilled fig, mint compote, and creamy riata, to name just a few.

The entrees are the "soul" of the restaurant. It is one of the few places where one can find venison, duck, rabbit, pheasant, quail, lamb, and seafood. The entrees are based on the season, and the menu changes quarterly. A special favorite is the Venison which is included in the winter selection. The Venison is wrapped in puff pastry with mushroom duxelle, served with autumn fruits and vegetables.

Spring offerings include A Tuna Tasting which is comprised of tuna prepared three incredible ways. Act 1 is the Tuna Tartare complemented with Wasabi-Lime Aioli, Act 2 is the Salad Nicoise with Herb Encrusted Seared Tuna, and Act 3 is the Seared Tuna served on Creamy Celeriac Puree.

The summer menu is just as unique! Feast on Wok Fried Whole Fresh Fish topped with a spicy Thai Chili sauce or Cowboy Veal Chop with Blackberry Demi-Glace.

If wild game is not your thing go for the steak menu. Food for the soul includes a Petite Chateau which includes several fillets wrapped in double smoked bacon served with green onion pancakes topped with Stilton blue cheese cream sauce and asparagus.

Maybe.... "Soul" in the name is appropriate. After all, when dinner was over, we felt that we had "died and gone to heaven".

Him: I hope they let me through the Pearly Gates.
Van: Fat chance!
Cat: Did you say I look fat?

Aqua Star (Westin Resort)
1 Resort Drive
912-201-2000

Although we often rave about the great views from the restaurants on River Street, another treat is eating across the river at the Aqua Star. Large windows look out on the Savannah River, and one can watch not only the boats going by, but also River Street and the city skyline.

The dining room has an understated nautical theme, with sea shells and model ships on display, along with unique glassware that is quite dramatic. The restaurant is known for its Sunday buffet breakfast, with omelets made to order, waffles, fruits, cheeses, assortments of breads, fresh local seafood, salad bar and other lunchtime dishes.

At dinner, warm bread with butter fruit nut spread begins the night, and is the setting for the delicious meal to come. For appetizers, we recommend the Portobello Mushroom, Lump Crab Cake (served with tomato okra roasted corn relish), Low Country Drizzle (skewers of shrimp, chicken and beef marinated in curry and ginger sauce), and the Signature She Crab Soup with sherry.

Recommended entrees include the Cedar-Planked Salmon (with port wine syrup), the Seafood Pot Pie (crab, shrimp, lobster, and scallops in berry salsa), and the Center Cut Black Angus Filet. A signature dish (for two) is the 5 Pound Maine Lobster which comes with salad, vegetable, and rice as well as pecan pie.

Dessert portions are huge! We especially liked the Carrot Cake (6 layers), Chef's Crème Brulee, Key Lime Pie (with mango coulis), Chocolate Mousse Torte, and Bread Pudding (with croissants and cranberries).

Part of the charm of dining at Aqua Star is taking the water taxi (available on River Street), which is full of romance and style. We guarantee that this dining adventure will shine bright in your memories of Savannah's fine dining constellation.

Cat: I love the view of River Street across the water!
Van: Isn't Savannah really beautiful?
Him: Hey, did you see that cool racing cigarette boat?

A Vida Restaurant & Wine Bar
113 W. Broughton Street
912-232-8432

If you desire an eclectic, unique dinner, then a Vida is the place to be ... da! Leave your claustrophobia at the door, the table next to you will become your new best friends! The tables are close, but fortunately, not to the point of intrusiveness. The decor is very 21st century, but it is intimate, warm, and inviting. The stainless steel bar is a great place to just sit and have a drink.

The menu is quite varied, but favorite appetizers include the Sesame Seared Tuna served with herbed sweet onion relish; the Golden Fried Calamari over spinach chiffonade, pepperoncinis and chili flakes; Roasted Nantucket Diver Scallops over wild mushrooms, truffle crème and citrus fruit; however, the MUST is the Jumbo Lump Crab Cake with orange-ginger aioli (No fillers here, the crab cake is all crab!). Try the Spinach Salad with blueberries, red onion, and almond griddled brie, served with mission fig vinaigrette.

For entrees we particularly suggest the Mesquite Grilled Chicken Breast with Roasted Tomato Parmesan Ziti, served with sautéed spinach and topped with a lime BBQ aioli. If you are hungry for seafood try the Bacon-Wrapped Salmon topped with crawfish béarnaise and served with mushroom pesto wild rice and grilled asparagus. Also, the tasty Beef Fillet needs special mention as it is served with pepper merlot caramel sauce and potato cakes with boursin cream sauce. All the entrees are served with different side dishes that are quite inventive and match perfectly to the meal.

A Vida is a Spanish toast "to life." And with the impressive wine selection, it's easy to make a lot of toasts. A Vida is a definite place to eat … da!

Him: I thought we were going to a shoe store!
Cat : Puhlease! That's Adida!
Van: This restaurant has to be seen to be believe-da!!!

B. Matthews
325 E. Bay Street
912-233-1319

If you want authentic, historic dining, B. Matthews is for you. Built in 1791, the restaurant has uneven wooden plank floors, giant timber pillars, and brick walls. While the ambience is old, the menu is very 21st. Century … creating a very Savannah dining experience.

A signature appetizer is the Black Eyed Pea Cake on mixed greens with spicy remoulade sauce, but it is rivaled by the Pancetta and Basil Wrapped Shrimp on cheesy grits with lemon butter. Green Apple and Vidalia Onion soup and the Crab Artichoke Fondue are also favorites among the locals.

Savannah is known for her seafood and B. Matthews accommodates with Pan Seared Salmon over creamy mustard spinach, pommes frittes, and brown butter caper sauce. If that is not to your palate, try the Tempura Grouper partnered with grilled andouille sausage, grilled white asparagus, red chili miso, and cilantro pesto. Kicking it up a notch, the Pecan Crusted Chicken with wild mushroom ravioli in chive tomato butter sauce, and the Braised Lamb with farfalle pasta in a rosemary scented parmesan broth will "sock it to ya!"

B. Matthews is also open for breakfast and serves a delicious array of pastries (try the Cinnamon Roll) as well as egg dishes, such as Quiches and French Toast. You can enjoy lunch here as well, with a variety of sandwiches and salads. You will find all the downtown locals sitting at the bar and tables. For y'all who are touring in Savannah, take a load off your feet and stop in for an afternoon libation! We guarantee, you will start with a drink, and end up staying for dinner!

Him: Can we drink all afternoon before we eat?
Cat: I'm ready for a black eyed Pea Cake!
Van: Can I give 'Him' a black eye?

Belford's
313 W. Saint Julian Street
912-233-2626

Belford's Seafood and Steaks, at 315 West Saint Julian Street in City Market is located in a building that originally housed Savannah's Hebrew Congregation. In pleasant weather we recommend sitting outside in the covered patio, however, inside the restaurant are floor-to-ceiling windows, wood planked floors, soaring ceilings, and brick walls, which make for a very romantic ambience.

Belford's serves excellent breakfasts, one of the few locations that are open in City Market in the morning. Try their Eggs Benedict, French Toast, Smoked Salmon Florentine and Blue Crab Frittata.

For appetizers, we recommend the Fried Calamari with spicy red chili sauce, She Crab Stew, and the Parmesan Tomato Stack (a baked combination of tomatoes, Parmesan and mozzarella cheese with vinaigrette). Highly recommended entrees are the Shrimp, Greens and Grits (shrimp with apple smoked bacon and Chardonnay sauce with fried grit triangles and wilted collard greens) and Crab Cake Entrée (with lemon aioli, spicy tomato jam, Savannah red rice and steamed asparagus). Incidentally, the Shrimp dish won the Best Entrée (2004) and the Crab dish won the Best Menu Item (2001) at the "Taste of Savannah," judged by *Southern Living Magazine*.

We also enjoyed the Georgia Pecan Grouper, Cajun Lobster Ravioli, Shrimp-stuffed Filet Mignon, and Hazelnut Red Snapper with crabmeat in a hazelnut liqueur sauce. We couldn't resist the desserts and can recommend Rum Bread Pudding, Fried Banana Cheesecake, and the Raspberry Chocolate Cheesecake.

Be sure to see some of the pictures that depict the area when Belford's Wholesale Foods was a bustling business.

Cat: Sitting outside is great for fresh air and people watching!
Van: I like the intimate charm of the inside of the restaurant.
Him: Hey, did you see what that horse just did? Pee-Yew!!! So much for your fresh air!

Boar's Head Grill and Tavern

1 N. Lincoln Street
912-651-9660

Step back in time and experience the feel of 18th century Savannah, while dining on the cuisine of the 21st century. The exposed brick walls are decorated with a collection of gold plates and hunting trophies. Chef Philip Branan, a CIA graduate and owner of the restaurant, provides entrees to delight even the most sophisticated palate. The focus is dining on locally-caught seafood, and shrimp is top on the menu. Try the Shrimp Fry, Shrimp Scampi, Stuffed Shrimp, Low Country Shrimp with Sausage and Cheese Grits, and Low Country Bouillabaisse (with fresh shrimp, of course!) The shrimp are succulent and tender and the seasonings are just right. Forrest Gump would be proud.

The Boar's Head also caters to the landlubber, as evidence by the bovine name. The steaks and chops are cooked to perfection and served with a choice of Bearnaise, Green Peppercorn, or Boar's Head Sauce, a secret sauce that if divulged, "I'd have to kill you!" The T-Bone Pork Chop was served with peach chutney and Garlic Mashed Potatoes.

The finishing touch is the home-made desserts that are well-worth the calories! Savannah Trifle Sponge Cake, soaked in Grand Marnier and topped with vanilla custard, whipped cream, and toasted almonds is sure to please as is the Chocolate Bread Pudding with Jack Daniels Sauce.

Afterward, a stroll along the Riverfront will be a wonderful ending to a delightful meal. The cobblestones, the ships sailing down the Savannah River, the smell of the ocean water and the sultry breeze will make it seem as if you are 'going back in time'.

Him: I thought that the restaurant would be boaring, but it was Great!
Van: Your humor is what is boring!
Cat: Can't we just talk about the wonderful food?

Carlito's

119 Martin Luther King Blvd
912-232-2525

Carlito's may be easy to miss, so look for the neon sign out front. The darkened windows and the small lobby area of the restaurant are deceptive, as they open up into a much larger area than one would expect. Booths are found down one side of the restaurant with the bar located on the other side. In between there are many tables that can easily be moved together for whatever size party you have.

The décor is authentic Mexican, with yellow walls, red booths and colorful wall paintings. Complimentary chips and cilantro-heavy salsa are served immediately while you study the huge menu. Most of the meals are typical Mexican-American fare. For those unaccustomed to Mexican food, there is a brochure on each table that lists the name in Spanish and provides a description of the food. The standard offerings, including tacos, tamales, quesadillas, burritos, and enchiladas are on the menu and are recommended. However, the fajitas are outstanding. The plates are served steaming hot, with grilled onions, bell peppers and pico de gallo as accompaniments. The Texas fajitas include a mix of beef, chicken and shrimp and are enough to satisfy any appetite.

All dishes arrive steaming hot and drinks are refilled often and without asking. They even serve "Southern iced tea" ... which of course means very sweet! Many of the waiters and waitresses appeared to be Hispanic, lending to the authenticity of the restaurant, and reflecting the growing Hispanic population of Savannah.

Even if it is not Cinco de Mayo, you can still enjoy good, inexpensive, authentic Mexican-American fare at Carlito's!

Him: Did somebody say Cinco de Mayo?
Van: Where's my sombrero?
Cat: Habla usted espanol?

Cha Bella Grill & Patio Bar
102 E. Broad Street
912-790-7888

Just mention the popular, Southern environmentally correct word "green" and the restaurant Cha Bella is immediately at the forefront.... fresh, local, and organic.

Cha Bella has both indoor and al fresco dining. The dining patio is warm and cozy, decorated with 13 foot palm trees, large swings, chandeliers, and 15 foot privacy curtains. The best part of the patio is the large screen, on which new and vintage movies are shown, Wednesday through Saturday, starting at 7 P.M. No longer do we have to eat stale popcorn, drink flat soda, and feel total embarrassment if our friends catch us in our pajamas for the family 'drive in movie night'! If dining outside is not to your liking, the inside is whimsical and romantic.

The menu is eclectic and is frequently changing but there are certain food favorites that remain constant, and include the rustic Flatbread Pizza's that are topped with wonderful combinations of vegetables, meat, and cheese; and the Fried Green Tomato Campanile, a stack of fried green tomatoes layered with goat cheese, lump crab meat, and drizzled with lobster remoulade.

The Zuppa Di Mare, a traditional Italian Christmas seafood soup, has been Southern-ized and consists of fettuccine noodles, a hot and spicy red wine tomato sauce and an ocean full of wild Georgia shrimp, scallops, calamari, and mussels. Cha Bella Grouper is sure to delight with fresh mango salsa and a serrano buerre blanc sauce. For the land lubber, the steaks and veal are sure to please!

IF (and that is a big IF) you have room for dessert, the Crème Brulee, Key Lime Cheesecake, or Chocolate Dipped Cannoli will definitely fill your caloric count for the day. What else can we say except Ciao, Y'all!

Cat: I love the combination of divine food and classic movies!
Him: Do they show cartoons before the movies?
Van: We can't take you anywhere!

Chart House
202 W. Bay Street
912-234-6686

The Chart House is a delightful place to spend a quiet evening. Part of a chain of restaurants, the Chart House has long been known for the prime rib and steaks, but have recently added seafood and fish dishes

The Chart House is in a former sugar and cotton warehouse that dates to 1790, and is one of the oldest masonry structures in Georgia. On a pleasant evening, try to get a seat on the covered outdoor deck that overlooks the Savannah River.

Delicious appetizers include a Crab, Avocado and Mango Stack, Seared Peppered Ahi Tuna (with ginger and wasabi) and Lobster Spring Rolls (with a mustard sauce). Or perhaps one would prefer the Clam Chowder (New England style) or Lobster Bisque (laced with sherry).

One of their specialties, the Prime Rib—Chart House Cut, is slow roasted and served au jus. The New York Strip, Tenderloin Medallions, and Filet Mignon are made from corn-fed beef, aged and char-grilled. Today's fish selection can be prepared anyway the diner prefers. Our recommended fish specialties include Snapper Hemingway (sautéed with lump crab and shallot butter), Dynamite Mahi Mahi (crab crusted with chive oil drizzle and coconut ginger rice) and Macadamia Crusted Mahi Mahi (peanut sauce with a hint of Frangelico, mango coulis and rice pilaf).

Your dinner at the Chart House can't be considered complete without their signature Hot Chocolate Lava Cake (a chocolate soufflé served warm, it requires 30 minute notice) or Original Mud Pie (they claim to have invented it!).

The Chart House offers a casual atmosphere with delicious food and great service, a great end to the day spent along River Street.

Cat: I love these old historic warehouses!
Van: I love all the decorative, directional charts on the walls.
Him: Decorations? I thought they were real directional charts! No wonder I got lost on the way to the men's room!

Clary's
404 Abercorn Street
912-233-0402

Clary's Café, at 404 Abercorn Street has been known as Savannah's favorite "greasy spoon" for over a century. Clary's was made even more famous by the movie *Midnight in the Garden of Good and Evil*, in which it posed as a drugstore, which was its former purpose. The Café has a 1950s diner motif, with a soda counter as well as tables and chairs.

No trip to Savannah is complete without having breakfast at Clary's. Your waitress is sure to call you "honey" and will put up with no nonsense. Don't be surprised if she slaps the menu down on the table and rolls her eyes at anything you say. It is definitely a down home atmosphere. The tables are crowded together, complete with many locals! Just sit back and enjoy the atmosphere.

The food choice is difficult, because there are so many options. We enjoyed the Malted Waffle (a huge Belgian Waffle) as well as Hoppel Poppel (scrambled eggs with salami, potatoes, onions and green peppers), Seafood Omelette (shrimp, scallops, Swiss cheese, and lobster sauce) and Crab Cakes Benedict. You also can't go wrong with the Biscuits and Gravy, or the buttermilk biscuits in any form … ham biscuit, egg biscuit, here a biscuit, there a biscuit … etc.! If you are really sampling the Southern breakfast, than the grits are also a 'must' and very delectable!!

For the sweet tooth, there are two items you simply must try. First, the Pecan Caramel Bun was huge, sticky and simply scrumptious. The Giant Éclair is indeed that. Nobody could finish one on his own, so be sure to share it.

Clary's also serves lunch that includes salads, sandwiches, and other Southern dishes. Note that they close at 4 PM, so don't show up for dinner.

Him: I closed my eyes and woke up in Mel's Diner!
Van: Yeah, where's Flo?
Cat: Well, kiss my grits!

Cobblestone Conch House

225 W. River Street
912-232-5551

The location of the Cobblestone Conch House can best be described as "overlooking the power plant"; however, once inside you will feel like you are on a beautiful island.

The restaurant has a Caribbean theme in both décor and menu, as evidenced by the pineapple light fixtures on the outside wall. One immediately feels the island influence with wood, bamboo and brick interior as well as tropical pictures on the walls.

The cuisine generally reflects the very popular Caribbean fare and it's hard to guess a major main ingredient. (Here's a hint, it starts with C and ends with h, and by the way, it rhymes with honk). The Conch Fritters are light, flavored with herbs and spices, and served with apricot chutney and lime remoulade sauce. Get "conched" on the head with the incredible Coconut Encrusted Shrimp, which are quite crunchy and perfectly prepared with lime remoulade sauce. Still hungry, mon?

The Conch House serves great seafood, as evidenced by the Jamaican Spice Seared Tuna (served over coconut rice with spicy orange mojo and mango salsa), the Whole Fried Snapper, Thai Basil Steamed Halibut, and Jamaican Beer Battered Shrimp. For the landlubber, try the house specialty, Churrasco (skirt steak marinated in chimichurri with marinated sweet onions and tomato cucumber salsa) served with scallion whipped potatoes and a trio of wonderful sauces that are tart, sweet, and soothing all at the same time! If the descriptions of the food do not wow you, the presentations certainly will!

Beg the chef to make the Banana Crème Brulee for the finale of the meal and while you are indulging get an after dinner drink at the "Hemingway-esque" bar. The rattan chairs, old fashioned palm fans, and palm trees will have you looking out the window hoping for a glimpse of "The Old Man and The Sea." I'll bet he never ate so good!

Him: I think I just saw Jimmy Buffet!
Van: No, that was Papa Hemingway.
Cat: No, it was the ghost of Bob Marley. I think we all ate the worm in the tequila!

Cotton Exchange Tavern
201 E. River Street
912-232-7088

This affordable, casual tavern occupies a former cotton warehouse that dates to the 18th century. Prices tend to be a little lower than some of the other eateries along River Street, especially for lunch. The menu is extensive, so you can always find something for everyone.

If you're fortunate enough to get a seat by a window, you can watch the comings and goings along the river as you enjoy beef and seafood selections, as well as a wide range of fish prepared to order. Lighter entrees are also available, plus famous sandwiches, soups and tavern fare appetizers.

Some appetizers you'll enjoy are the Tybee Crab Chowder which is thick with crabmeat and potatoes and corn, the Crab Cakes, and Fried Green Tomatoes. All of their soups are homemade and delicious, so you can't go wrong with any of them.

Recommended entrees include the New York Strip Steak, the Black and Blue Rib eye (with Cajun spices), the Shrimp Trio (bacon-wrapped, fried and garlic shrimp) and the Fried Seafood Platter. The Shrimp and Grits had at least a dozen shrimp, with a fried grit cake, but the sauce was disappointing with very little flavor.

As mentioned above, you can enjoy an inexpensive lunch here, as they have a variety of sandwiches and salads and a large burger selection. We recommend the Black and Blue Burger, Cajun Shrimp Salad, Cajun Pasta, Crab Salad Sandwich, and the Sea Island Sub. Make sure you try the potato salad, as it is the best in town! Desserts we liked were the Snicker Pie, the Bourbon Pecan Pie and the Chocolate Trifle.

The Cotton Exchange Tavern has a very casual atmosphere and customers include families as well as groups of adults.

Van: This is one of the best places in town for lunch.
Cat: I particularly like their Reuben Sandwiches.
Him: How much cotton do you need to exchange for a steak?

Courtyard Café

601 East Bay Street
912-238-1200

If you're looking for a varied and sizeable meal, go to the Courtyard Café at the Mulberry Inn for their Southern-style breakfast buffet and lunch buffet. Dinner is served off the menu with selections including steaks, seafood, pasta, sandwiches and nightly specials.

The Courtyard Cafe overlooks a lavishly landscaped courtyard, surrounded by greens and beautiful flowers overlooking quaint balconies and peaceful surroundings. The Café is bright and cheerful, with lots of windows for good lighting, and soft music playing in the background.

The Mulberry Inn serves a scrumptious Southern-style breakfast buffet daily or you may prefer to order a la carte. The buffet includes eggs, sausage, grits and gravy, biscuits, and assorted other breads. Another bountiful Southern-style buffet is available at lunch. The varied menu depending on the day will include: shrimp and corn bisque, baked chicken, lasagna, fried catfish, mashed potatoes, corn, and cabbage, fix-it-yourself-salad, fried chicken, fried fish, liver and onions, whipped potatoes, squash casserole, and lima beans. It is all-you-can eat, so prepare to go off the diet!! Although one can order from the menu, our recommendation is to go through the buffet.

Make sure you take some time to look around the Mulberry Hotel. The period furnishings, oil paintings, polished hardwood floors, and elegant chandeliers make you feel you are in the Historic District of Savannah. A "Southern Tradition" at the Mulberry Inn is their unique "Tea Time." They serve delicious dessert treats and afternoon teas while you can listen to live piano music from 4:00 PM until 6:00 PM daily.

The Courtyard Café is a pleasant escape from a hectic day, and the buffet can fill you up completely.

Him: I now know how pregnant women feel!
Cat: Welcome to the world!!!
Van: Do you think he will go through penopause?

Firefly Café
321 Habersham Street
912-234-1971

If you want to taste of the ambience of Savannah, you can't find a better place than the Firefly Café on Troup Square.

The Firefly sits at the intersection of Habersham and Harris and has both indoor and outdoor dining. In good weather, there is no better place to enjoy the sunshine and outdoors. In the summer heat or winter cold, one might opt for indoor seating instead. Tables indoors seat either two or four people, and the area is fairly small, so it is not recommended for large parties. There is music playing indoors, and the walls are decorated with artwork from local galleries.

Some excellent appetizers include Corn Chowder (with corn, red-skinned potatoes, and carrots in a creamy sauce) and the Caribbean Shrimp (which has a bite to it). A light alternative would be the Cranberry Pecan Salad with spinach, craisins, pecans, and jicama or the Grilled Salmon Club Sandwich with bacon, tomato and lettuce on a croissant. For entrees, the Atlantic Salmon (served with sweet corn pecan hash), the Troup Square Pasta (shrimp, asparagus, tomatoes, and basil served over linguine) and the Grilled Pork Chop (served with garlic mashed potatoes and Granny Smith applesauce). For dessert, the Southern Comfort Peach Bread Pudding (with vanilla ice cream) can't be beat.

The Firefly also serves excellent breakfasts, including the Eggs Benedict (with crab and grits), the Blueberry-Corn Pancakes, the Crabmeat and Spinach Omelet, and the Greek Omelet. If it is lunch or brunch, be sure to try the Cranberry Pecan Spinach Salad, a unique blend of flavors.

The Firefly definitely shines among the small intimate eateries of Savannah. The food is as bright as the name suggests!

Cat: What a beautiful, peaceful setting!
Him: I'm going to catch some fireflies in my jar!
Van: Oh … put a lid on it!

Garibaldi's

315 West Congress Street
912-232-7118

Savannah is known for fine Southern Cuisine, so who would think that Savannah would have an incredible authentic Italian Restaurant. Somehow, Garibaldi's has achieved this by fusing Italian flair with Southern specialties, and the result is "Bellisimo!"

Garibaldi's was originally a firehouse, and the rustic ambience makes for a sophisticated dining experience. The dress is casual chic, but elastic waste bands are suggested!!! At times the noise level can be somewhat daunting, but it is also energizing and fun.

Shrimp Savannah is a great beginning, with lightly, sautéed shrimp served with Pernod cream sauce, made all the better when sopped up with the crusty garlic bread. The Shrimp Risotto Cakes sautéed with country ham and cream are a close second place followed by Denver Lamb Ribs with sweet ginger, soy, and pear cabbage relish. For the diet conscious, the Raw and Steam Bar provides calorie-conscious appetizers.

A Daily Specials board provides quite an impressive array of entrees and one never goes wrong when choosing from this list. It generally includes fresh local fish, beef, veal, and pasta dishes. Several favorites are the Veal Chop Au Poire served with wild mushroom brandy sauces, Crispy Scored Flounder served with an apricot-shallot glaze, and Lobster Pasta. The chef definitely has flair with food combinations, thus making this restaurant a favorite among locals. The "after dinner" menu speaks highly of Garibaldi's attention to the complete dining experience. This includes desserts and aged port, sherry and cognacs. Added treats are the dessert martinis, which include the Chocolate Martini, the Creme-Brulee Martini, and the Hazelnut Latte.

As Savannah has survived the "test of time" (est. 1733), so has Garibaldi's. It just goes to show you that the BEST do last ... and sometimes come in first!

Him: Do they still have fire trucks?
Van: Who cares about the fire trucks? Where are the firemen?
Cat: Augh! Time for another martini!

Huey's on the River
115 East River Street
912-234-7385

Huey's on the River offers some of the best people-watching sites in Savannah (from the floor-to-ceiling windows facing River Street) and some of the best Cajun fare east of NOLA (New Orleans, Louisiana, for you non-travelers)!

Huey's specializes in seafood, but also has traditional New Orleans fare. The specialties of the house (all are recommended) include the Pasta Jambalaya (with Andouille sausage, chicken, and shrimp sautéed in Creole sauce and served over linguini), Shrimp and Scallop Thermidor (Shrimp and Scallops sautéed in Lobster sauce and served over linguini), and Shrimp and Grits (shrimp on a bed of grits in special Cajun sauce). The traditional Louisiana favorites include Shrimp Creole, Crawfish Etoufee, Red Beans and Rice, Muffulettas, and Po'boys and are also highly recommended. Don't forget to try the delicious, almost cake-like cornbread that is served with meals. The one disappointment was the side salad served with dinner: the iceberg lettuce with grated cheese and tiny croutons had very little flavor and would have enhanced the meal if field greens were used instead.

Huey's is also well known for its breakfasts that include Eggs Benedict, Eggs Blackstone (Benedict, but served with a grilled Beefsteak tomato), Eggs Sardou (Benedict with creamed spinach and artichoke hearts) and Pain Perdue (New Orleans style French toast). New Orleans-style omelettes are also available and of course the "world famous" beignets.

The beignets taste just like the ones served at the Café DuMonde in New Orleans. The only difference is that you will not have a powdered sugar bath! In addition to the beignets, one can also enjoy the Praline Cheesecake or Chocolate Turtle Cheesecake for the end of the meal.

Him: I guar-an-damn-tee this is the best!
Van Emeril must be the chef.
Cat: Do I look good with a powdered sugar bath?

Il Pasticcio
2 East Broughton (at the corner of Bull)
912-231-8888

Il Pasticcio, which means "joyful chaos", is owned by Pino Venetico, who was born in Sicily. Venetico turned this former Lerner store into an upscale restaurant with high ceilings and a bistro-like atmosphere. Windows look out on the street on two sides of the restaurant, which makes for great people-watching.

The restaurant has an exposed kitchen, allowing for interesting chef voyeurism and a peek into great kitchen antics (Thanks to Hells Kitchen). However, the sounds from the kitchen, the high ceilings, and the number of people in the restaurant create a very high level of noise.

USA Today recently rated the restaurant as one of the top 10 Italian restaurants in the U.S. We certainly agree with that rating. The menu contains a number of savory options, so we had a hard time making up our minds. However, we can recommend the Grilled Salmon with potato and pancetta gratin, and the Grilled Filet Mignon topped with Gorgonzola and served with a gratin of potatoes and pancetta along with caramelized onions and vegetables. We also recommend the Grilled Rack of Lamb served with sautéed spinach and roasted potatoes in a port reduction.

The pasta dishes are also notable. The Capellini Con Scampi, Capesante, Funghi E Zafferano (angel hair pasta sautéed with shrimp, sea scallops, mushrooms, crushed red pepper and tomatoes in a saffron sauce) will fill you up, but we also recommend Ravioli Alle Noci, which is homemade spinach ravioli tossed in a creamy walnut sauce.

Him: This tasted a LOT better than my spaghetti with Ragu sauce!
Van: O, Solo Mio!
Cat: Is Gordon Ramsey in the kitchen?

Isaac's at 9 Drayton

9 Drayton Street
912-231-0100

Isaac's, in the old Churchill's location and a local favorite, is worth a visit. The massive bar, which survived the Churchill's fire, was imported from England and still stands like royalty as the prize showpiece here. Also, in the main dining area is a framed boxing glove belonging to Muhammad Ali. In times past, this spot served as a boxing ring, where tales have it a local boxer was "snuffed out." The townspeople were said to have hanged the murderer in the basement of this building. Ghost tales say that someone can still be seen hanging in the basement late at night. Upstairs is a private dining room, appropriately, with a picture of scenes from *The Sopranos* series. Rooftop dining is available in good weather.

To start off, we suggest the Sugar Cane Skewered Moroccan Chicken with Tzatziki dressing, Grilled Shrimp & Fried Green Napoleon with red pepper remoulade, and Grilled Shrimp & Polenta Cake with Tasson Ham, chive, and Asiago cream sauce. As an entrée, we can recommend the Grouper with Yukon smashed potatoes and seasonal veggies. The Seafood Pasta with Cream Sauce is delicate and not too heavy. In one corner, ready to duke it out for a win, is the Beggar's Purse which consists of a chicken breast, baby collards and garlic boursin cheese, delicately wrapped in phyllo pastry tied with a leek bow and baked. And in the other corner, is Herbed Pork Tenderloin with mushroom brandy cream sauce served atop a sweet potato cake. It might just be a draw!

The restaurant offers live music Thursday through Saturday evenings. You have to try their Mojito and Pomegranate Martini.

All in all, this place is a knock out!

Van: Let's put in an order of mussels (muscles) for Him.
Cat: I don't think even that will help.
Him: Yo, Adrienne, a drink!
Van & Cat: Yo, Adrienne, let him get it himself!

Jazz'd

52 Barnard St.
912-236-7777

One of our favorite spots for dinner downtown is Jazz'd.

Jazz'd Tapas Bar is located in the old Kress Building, or as many people say, under the Gap (clothing retailer). A tapas restaurant serves small portions of what are normally offered as entrees in other restaurants. The normal practice when several people are dining is to order a number of different "tapas" and share within the group.

The restaurant is located in the basement, so one might expect that it would be dark. However, each of the tables has a bright light over it, directing the rays down on the table. The décor is "very hip-cool-trendy-happening-colorful and artsy." A rather unusual wine storage area greets visitors, so be sure to check out the many labels that are stocked. Each of the walls is painted a different color that includes lime, coral, teal, and citron and to complement the lively color scheme, local artwork is displayed.

The small portion of tapas encourages sharing and makes for great "grazing." Recommended are: Creole Style Tomato Dip with Goat Cheese, Conch Fritters, Calamari with Sweet Bananas, Martini Marinated Tenderloin Tips, Crab Cakes with Shrimp Sauce, Cuban Rubbed Beef Satays (with sweet pepper glaze on skewers), Macadamia Nut Crusted Ahi with chutney, Beer-Battered Portobello Mushroom with horseradish sauce and Skewered Barbecue Shrimp and Grits. You can also try the Tapas for Two option in which you each get soup or salad, four tapas of your choice and two desserts.

Desserts change every day, but the Bread Pudding, Irish Cream Pie and the Dark Chocolate Torte are definitely curtain calls.

A unique treat, Jazz'd Tapas Bar will make Louis Armstrong proud!

Him: Did I just see Wynton Marsalis?
Van: Keep looking, so we can eat your share.
Cat: We need another table for all our food!

Lady and Sons
102 West Congress
912-233-2600

The latest and greatest Savannah icon is a petite fire ball of Southern charm who can hold her own with both the sass of Scarlet O'Hara and the cooking skills of Mammy.

Paula Deen is a tribute to those who have tenacity, motivation, and maybe even a small amount of wackiness. She began the restaurant business with her two sons in the late 1980s as a venture known as "The Bag Lady". They delivered the best business lunches known to mankind, direct to the office, the board room, or to those simply stuck at their desks. Needless to say the rest is history.

Paula and her two son's are now the proud proprietors of The Lady and Sons Restaurant. This restaurant offers the finest example of down-home Southern cooking, so don't plan on getting your cholesterol checked in the days following. Instead, plan of feeling like you "Frankly don't give a damn!"

The well known buffet is an absolute steal and will leave you ready for a nap afterward. It includes Fried Chicken, Collard Greens, Pork Ribs, Low Country Boil, Macaroni and Cheese, Black Eyed Pea's, Potatoes, Creamed Corn, Sweet Potato Hoe Cakes.... come on down y'all!

If the buffet is not to your liking, then by all means, plan on pleasing your palate with the menu selections. Paula and her sons have been a well known secret in Savannah for years. Not since Julia Childs and French Cuisine has there been a personality that has combined regional cooking with a culinary expertise as Paula Deen has with Dixie Land.

All we can figure is, "As God is my witness, I will never be hungry again".

Cat: How did Scarlett have a 16 inch waist with food like this?
Van: Do I look pregnant?
Him: I ain't birthin' no babies!

Local 11 Ten
1110 Bull Street
912-790-9000

Savannah is nationally known for southern hospitality, but inherent in the southern culture is the pride of being a Savannian. Local 11 Ten started with the thought of being a "local hang-out restaurant," but the word quickly got out that this was more than a corner eatery, and instead was a restaurant of the highest caliber. It has raised the culinary notch of dining in Savannah, and the Chef's daily specials are equal to any cuisine in the major food capitals. It is also known for the never empty wine glass!

Local 11 Ten has both small plates, and starters. Small plates are designed to provide tastes for each individual at the table, which is a great idea for an introduction of the excellent food to come. Steak Tartare, Pork and Veal Meatballs, Wild Georgia Shrimp Sautéed with Garlic, are to name but a few of the delicacies to be savored. The starters are next! Red Snapper, sliced extremely thin, is served atop pickled fennel, greens, and crispy rosemary and basil oil. Another local favorite is the Grilled Quail with spinach, pine nuts, gorgonzola, figs, and warm bacon vinaigrette. The selections change daily according to season and the availability of local ingredients, but know that the chef is a genius and will create a masterpiece to please!

Main courses that are 'local' favorites include: Grilled Black Grouper with fregola pasta, butternut squash, Brussels sprouts, pancetta, and green apple curry sauce; and Grilled Berkshire Pork Chop with spinach, roasted fennel, and boulangere potatoes. A personal favorite is the Grilled Hanger Steak with Yukon gold potato puree, haricot vert, tomato and bordelaise sauce.

Saving room for dessert is an absolute necessity! The Chocolate, consisting of pots de crème, chocolate sorbet, and flourless chocolate cake will melt in your mouth (and not in your hand!), and the Brioche Bread Pudding served with caramelized apples, butter rum sauce, and maple ice cream will be the lightest bread pudding you've ever enjoyed

The staff is attentive, unobtrusive, and very diligent in attending to every detail, which makes the dining experience a truly memorable experience. We're glad that we are "locals!"

Him: Is Local 11 Ten a union?
Van: I'm all about the never ending wine glass!
Cat: I'll have the desserts please, two of each!

Magnolia Restaurant

15 East Liberty Street
912-232-9000

The Magnolia Restaurant, located in the DeSoto Hilton Hotel offers authentic Southern cuisine and local specialties. Perhaps best known for its Sunday and holiday buffets, the hotel offers a Low Country buffet at both breakfast and lunch Monday through Saturday. The buffet includes Southern favorites such as Crab Cakes, Fried Chicken, Grits and Fried Green Tomatoes. Additionally, champagne is served with the Sunday brunch. They are also well known for their holiday brunches (i.e. Christmas, Easter, and Mother's Day).

The hotel has underground parking, with entry from Liberty Street. With a meal in the Magnolia, you can have your parking ticket validated. Unfortunately, with it being right off the lobby, as so often happens in hotel restaurants, voices and noises from the lobby can disturb the ambiance of the dining room. Even the soft jazz music can't overcome the crowd noises at times. However, the room has been beautifully restored and brings to mind Southern elegance.

Appetizers we recommend include the Pork Won Ton, Crab Cakes, Coconut Shrimp, and Grilled Baby Marinated Lamb Chops. The bread basket includes homemade rolls that are delicious and hard to turn down.

The menu has a number of "Healthy Menu" items that are designated, so those having special dietary needs can be easily accommodated. We particularly liked (<u>not</u> from the healthy menu!) the Southern Shrimp and Grits (with fried green tomatoes), Pan-Seared Chilean Sea Bass, Braised Veal Shank Osso Bucco, and Sesame-Crusted Tuna.

Desserts we can suggest include the Chocolate Pyramid Anglaise and Tiramisu.

For contemporary Southern cuisine in a beautifully restored grand dining room, stop for dinner at the Magnolia Restaurant.

Van: Even the name, Magnolia, makes you think of Southern hospitality
Him: Magnolia. Isn't that the boat the Pilgrims came over on?
Cat: That was the Mayflower, idiot!

Mrs. Wilkes Dining Room

107 W. Jones Street
912-232-2599

Mrs. Wilkes was the quintessential classic Southern lady who turned a boarding house into a renowned family-style eatery, and she will always be associated with Southern gentility at its best. The Savannah sky darkened the day that Mrs. Wilkes passed; however, the sun rose with a new generation of Wilkes and the tradition lives on!

No visit to Savannah is complete without breakfast or lunch at Mrs. Wilkes. The restaurant is located in a historic townhouse on Jones Street. One can easily spot it by the long line winding down the street. The meals are served family-style and are infused with Southern hospitality. It is not unusual to see guests wander to the kitchen (perhaps to try to steal a secret recipe) or just to watch cooking at its best.

The meals are served family style, so prepare to make new friends and have a wonderful time! A prayer begins the meal, usually led by a member of the Wilkes's family. Following this, the parade of food begins: Roast Pork, Fried Chicken, Pot Roast, Ham, Macaroni and Cheese, Black Eyed Peas, Collard Greens, Okra, Mashed Potatoes, and of course, home-made Biscuits and Gravy. If one of the dishes are emptied, just ask for more. And, yes, Virginia, there is dessert: Pound Cake, Banana Pudding, and other Southern Delicacies.

The "Amen" to this meal is a loosening of the belt and an afternoon nap. How much better can it get?

Van: The epitome of true, down-home cooking!
Him: I knew Mrs. Wilkes—She's the mama of Ashley Wilkes, married to Melody Wilkes—over by Tara.
Cat: I'm surprised you could read the book. Oh, wait; you probably just saw the movie!

Olde Pink House

23 Abercorn Street
912-232-4286

No trip to Savannah is complete without a visit to the Olde Pink House on Reynolds Square. Built in 1771 for James Habersham Jr., this bright pink house (caused by antique bricks showing through a coating of stucco) has served several functions: private home, bank, and even headquarters for Sherman's generals.

The service was exemplary, from beginning to end. We did not have a reservation, but we highly recommend it.

We were immediately served with their small corn muffins and yeast rolls for munching while perusing the menu. Appetizers are a must, and we recommend several: Fried Green Tomatos, and sautéed shrimp with grits cakes and ham. Although salads are offered (the mixed field greens with gorgonzola cheese and champagne vinaigrette was delicious), we suggest skipping those, ordering just an entrée and saving room for dessert.

Recommended entrées include the Crispy Scored Flounder with apricot sauce, Blackened Grouper stuffed with Blue Crab served with Vidalia onion sauce, Grilled Tenderloin of Pork crusted with almonds and molasses, and the Tilapia Special. Our favorite dessert is the Praline Basket filled with vanilla ice cream and mango sauce.

Dinner can be served in the basement (Planters Tavern), but even for those who eat in the main house, you ought to consider an after dinner drink in the basement which has stone walls and beams with gas fireplaces and piano entertainment. When making reservations, be sure to ask for an upstairs table with a window that overlooks the square.

This restaurant is a favorite with tourists but locals visit on special occasions. One can dine in casual clothes, yet still feel that it is a formal with settings of linen tablecloths, candlelight, and high ceilings.

This is truly a memorable meal ... romantic, sensual, and full of history. Once again, ask your server about the resident ghost. He is known to turn the pictures around, and to eat the Trifle when the restaurant is closed.

Him: Real men DO eat in Pink Houses!
Van: Where is there a real man?
Cat: When you find him, he is mine!

Olympia Café

5 East River Street
912-233-3131

We all loved the movie "My Big Fat Greek Wedding," and the origin could have come from the Olympia Café! Start with the Ouzo (a licorice-flavored alcohol) and get ready to dance on the tables!

As appetizers, we can recommend the Tiropitakia (bite-sized triangles of phyllo dough and feta cheese), Saganaki (flamed brandy-topped cheese to dip pita bread in), Skordalia (a combination of garlic, mashed potatoes, olive oil and vinegar), Kalamarakia (calamari), and Hummus (chickpeas and sesame seed paste).

A number of traditional Greek dishes make the choosing difficult for an entrée and include; Spanakotiropita (spinach and feta cheese in phyllo dough), Dolmades (grape leaves stuffed with ground lamb and rice), Moussaka (baked eggplant) and Pastitsio (baked dish consisting of pasta, ground lamb, grated cheese, tomatoes, and cinnamon). Other dishes served Greek style include Shrimp Aegean (in a light marinara sauce over pasta with feta cheese), Lamb Chops (marinated and char-grilled with oven potatoes), Souvlaki (lamb shish-kebob), and Lemon Chicken.

No Greek meal is complete without some Baklava to finish it off. The dessert is layers of phyllo dough with honey, chopped nuts, and total decadence.... not to mention calories ... but, at this point, who is counting?
As we all saw in the movie, Greek food is a very important aspect of the Greek culture and family. Olympia Café does not disappoint! OPA!!!!

Him: Did you know that I'm Greek?
Van: Really? I thought you were Geek!
Cat: Another double Ouzo please!

Pirates' House
20 East Broad Street
912-233-5757

James Oglethorpe, after arriving in Savannah, planted a historical garden which he named the Trustees' Garden. This garden was experimental and consisted of 10 acres with plants from around the world.

After the need for the garden no longer existed, the Pirates' House was built. Initially it was an Inn for visiting seamen and it rose in popularity to become one of the favored meeting places for unsavory pirates and sailors. Supposedly there is an underground tunnel leading from one of the rooms to the river front, where allegedly, drunken men were shanghaied to serve aboard a ship, only to realize that when they awoke, it was unfortunately many miles from shore. It is also still known to be the home of many ghosts; most notably, Captain Flint of Treasure Island fame.

There are 15 dining rooms and all have the ambience of the historical pirate era. The menu reflects hearty Southern fare and includes Shrimp and Grits, She Crab Soup, Grilled Jumbo Shrimp, and Oven Fried Green Tomatoes. A main course fit for any pirate is the Seafood Harvest Platter—a hearty offering of fried shrimp, oysters, scallops and Tilapia. A Savannah favorite is the infamous Southern Honey Pecan Fried Chicken, which according to pirate lore is "to die for!" Maybe some of the pirates did!

Not to be outdone by any pirate booty, the Pirates' House also offers a daily buffet of endless desserts that is a treasure to behold. A favorite with families, this eatery is geared to the younger pirate wanna-be.

So, get your eye patch, find your old ruffled shirt and start practicing—"Ahoy, Mate"—you will definitely find your treasure at the Pirates' House.

Him: Did you see that cake disappear? I think the ghost ate it!
Cat: Don't look now, but I'm going to make another piece disappear.
Van: How can we make "Him" disappear?

River House Seafood

125 West River Street
912-234-1900

Located on the ground floor of a 1850s King Cotton Warehouse, the River House features brick walls, beamed ceilings, paintings of the port, and windows that look out on River Street.

If you're in the mood for imbibing, try their famous Chatham Artillery Punch (which involves wine, rum, whiskey, gin, brandy and champagne and comes with a souvenir glass), and will possibly make you feel that you are on the river rather than beside the river! Have the delicious Rosemary-Potato Bread and it will get you back to shore!

The Savannah Crab Cake (with mango chutney), Grilled Scallops (with a fan of asparagus) and Lobster Crab Bisque are each a great beginning to your meal. Specialties of the house include Pecan Encrusted Tilapia (with grits and zucchini), Mahi Mahi Blackened (on angel hair pasta), Cheryl Anne's Salmon (with whipped potatoes and caramelized onions), Pork Chop Jamaican, and Sirloin Au Poivre (with whipped potatoes and a burgundy sauce). Each of the entrees comes with a Caesar salad that is prepared table-side.

Don't forget to save room for dessert. All desserts are made at the on-site bakery and can be seen when one enters the restaurant. Our favorites are the Chocolate Cheesecake (a Savannah original), Georgia Pecan Pie, and Crème Brulee.

When one "returns," it is usually to go home. When one visits River Street, it is incomplete without a visit to The River House. You will feel like you are home when you eat at The River House!

Cat: I've never seen such beautiful desserts.
Van: Forget calorie counting tonight!
Him: I didn't know that calories could count!

Sapphire Grill
110 West Congress Street
912-443-9962

The Sapphire Grill is known as the 'gem 'of Savannah, both in name and cuisine. It has earned the designation of being the most romantic restaurant of Savannah, and many couples have become engaged while dining at the Sapphire Grill; thus, it has become the "Hope Diamond" of the fine dining establishments.

The atmosphere at the Sapphire Grill is intimate, cozy, and very private. There are several levels, decorated with Savannah gray brick, sapphire colors and bold art.

As with any gem, food is of the highest quality! Start with the wonderful Jumbo Lump Crab Cake with caper coral aioli and lobster oil. If that doesn't fit your fancy, order Lobster En Brioche with lemon mayonnaise and pea tendril salad.

Keep excellence going by ordering any one of the incredible entrees. A favorite is the Crisp Seared Tuna with creamy grits, preserved tomato, flash-seared heirloom arugula and wasabi. If you want to regress to childhood order the Rosemary and Shallot Spiked Colorado Lamb Lollipops (Okay, these are adult lollipops!) served with golden potato sage pancakes, rutabaga puree and cranberry oil. There is also a Chef's Testing Table, a meal that is considered to be a sparkling gem (please order in advance).

But.... there is more. If the entrees do not temp you, then order from the Grill. It consists of Prime Steaks, Poultry, Chops, and Prime Grilled Seafood (Tuna, Grouper, Salmon, Scallops, and Shrimp.) There are a variety of incredible sauces from which you can choose and personalize to your own liking.

The chef has been featured in the *New York Times, Southern Living, Bon Appetit, W Magazine, Food Network* and many more publications. For a true night of Old Savannah, complete with sultry Southern ambience, plan on going for the golden ring.... made complete with a "Sapphire" of course!

Cat: The Sapphire is my favorite stone.
Van: And now, it is my favorite food!
Him: Do they make cubic zirconium sapphires?

Season's Asian Bistro

125 East Broughton Street
912-238-8228

Visit the Orient without leaving Broughton Street by dining at Season's Asian Bistro. The Asian Bistro offers authentic Pan-Asian cuisine, featuring standard and exotic fare from across Asia. The restaurant is located in what once was the Old Avon Theater and later became the old City Lights Theater.

On stepping into the restaurant, diners are immediately transported to the Far East. At the back of the restaurant, a wall with water cascading down creates a calming effect. The Zen-like accents, palm-like fans, bamboo plants, colorful paintings and subdued lighting balance a contemporary sense of style and atmosphere.

The menu offers true Pan-Asian cuisine, with dishes from Japan and China, as well as Thailand, Korea, Malaysia, India, and Vietnam. This is a great place to share dishes in the tradition of Asian countries. One warning to the faint of heart, more than half of the dishes are designated as "spicy," so use caution in your selections or be prepared to use the fire extinguishers!

For appetizers, we can recommend the Nagiri and Maki Sushi, along with the Edamame (soybeans), Spring Rolls, and Shrimp Oujo. Suggested entrees include Thai Green Curry, Curried Tofu Hotpot, Stuffed Mango, and Sambal Asparagus with Seafood. Make sure you order the Green Tea, a pleasant complement to the spicy dishes. Savvy diners will save room for dessert, as the Coconut and Mango Ice Creams are a great way to finish the meal.

When you're undecided: "Chinese, Japanese, Thai, Malaysian, Korean, Indian—What shall it be," Season's Asian Bistro has something to satisfy all palates.

Cat: This is a great place to sample a variety of cuisines.
Him: I ate something that was so hot my face feels like Red China!
Van: Can we throw him off The Great Wall?

Shrimp Factory

313 East River Street
912-236-4229

The Shrimp Factory is definitely THE place for shrimp in Savannah. Reading the menu brings back memories of Bubba in Forrest Gump when he names all the shrimp dishes.

The Shrimp Factory has a bright red and white awning, so it is easy to spot. Like many of the other restaurants on River Street, it is housed in a 1890s building and served as a warehouse for cotton, resin and other products. The wooden beams, stones, and exposed-brick walls are the originals, while nautical items adorn the walls.

The Chatham Artillery Punch, a combination of gin, rum, champagne and brandy is served here, so if you're out for a celebration, try it. For those brave enough to prepare this concoction at home, the recipe is on the placemat.

The most popular dish is the Shrimp Stuffed Savannah (shrimp stuffed with deviled crab), which offers 8 shrimp, plentiful crab and a serving of rice. If you're really hungry, try the Pine Bark Stew, a bouillabaisse of shrimp, flounder, crab, oysters, potatoes and onions served in an iron pot with a bottle of sherry on the side. Other favorites include Pecan Crusted Flounder, Shrimp Fry, Shrimp and Crab Au Gratin, Shrimp Creole and Deviled Crab with mango curry chutney sauce. All entrees come with a delicious Caesar salad that is prepared tableside as well as Artisan Bread with a delicious cheddar cheese spread. The restaurant offers a daily Early Bird Special, a regular menu item priced below the normal.

For dessert we recommend Chocolate Coconut Cream Pie, Banana Bread Pudding, Bourbon Pecan Pie, and Key Lime Pie.

Him: Did Bubba Gump make all these shrimp dishes?
Van: Sure, why don't you go back to the kitchen and talk with him?
Cat: I think he and Bubba Gump will relate very well.

Skyler's

225 East Bay Street
912-232-3955

Skyler's Restaurant is in the cellar of the East Bay Inn, which was built in 1853 as a cotton warehouse. Skyler's shares the quaint décor of the Inn with its brick walls, high ceiling, exposed beams, fireplace and brick flooring, hinting of "Old Savannah" atmosphere. After passing through hotel lobby and cafe where bed and breakfast guests are served breakfast, one enters the restaurant by descending a winding staircase.

Many of the appetizers have the flavor of the Orient, so try the Moon Dim Sun which is shrimp and pork in wonton skins, served either fried or steamed. We also recommend one of our favorites, the Potsticker, which is a type of dumpling that is stuffed with pork and shrimp and lightly fried, served with soy and ginger dip.

A chalkboard on the landing details the specials of the day, which included Tomato-Crab Bisque and Blackened Grouper at one visit. The stand-out entree, however, was the Savannah Crab Cakes. They are lightly sautéed, with very little except crab as ingredients and as one diner proclaimed, "the best I have ever had!" In fact, Skyler's was voted as the "Best Crab Cakes" in a recent *Savannah Magazine* survey.

Another tasty dish is the Crispy Scored Flounder served with a light ginger sauce. You can't go wrong with one of their Stir-Fry dishes either. We particularly like the Garlic Chicken and Eggplant stir-fry, which is very flavorful. If chicken is your preference, try the Chicken Parmesan, absolutely delicious!

If you feel really indulgent, try the Éclair Cake for dessert!

For the cozy, warm feeling of Southern hospitality (and delectable crab cakes), Skyler's can't be beat.

Him: Why is "sky" in the title when it is in the basement?
Van: Hey, I know what it could be called—Cellar's

Cat: This is absolutely the last time I'm eating with you two!

Soho South Café

12 West Liberty Street
912-233-1633

The Soho South Café in the downtown area offers unusual dishes in a rather eclectic atmosphere. In addition to the restaurant, it includes an art gallery, used book store, coffee shop, and bakery. The walls of the restaurant are covered with paintings that are for sale, and before or after the meal one can stroll through these galleys and shop for paintings and other gift items. It originally was a car dealership, and the dining room was the garage.

Appetizers that are particularly unique include the rich and savory Tomato Basil Bisque and Bacon Wrapped Shrimp (Shrimp stuffed with pepper jack cheese, wrapped in bacon, broiled and served with Jezebel sauce). Yum!

For entrees, we suggest Sautéed Jumbo Lump Crabcakes, Stuffed Pork Tenderloin (served with apple jack sauce), Salmon Wellington (salmon, spinach and feta cheese in puff pastry with mustard-dill sauce), and Pepper Crusted Filet Mignon (with Madeira sauce). Each of these dishes is served with whipped potatoes, potatoes au gratin, or orzo-rice pilaf and a vegetable).

The restaurant also serves lunch daily with unusual combinations. We can recommend the Salmon BLT sandwich, Apple Walnut Chicken Salad, and Ham and Brie on Croissant. Some of these same dishes are found on the Sunday brunch menu along with traditional breakfast fare such as Southwestern Breakfast Casserole, Brioche French Toast (stuffed with fruit and cream cheese), and a Crisp Belgian Waffle. The outstanding breakfast fare, however, is Eggs Savannah (two crab cakes on a homemade biscuit with poached egg and hollandaise sauce, with asparagus and grits).

Be aware that refills on sodas are not free, since they fill the glasses from canned drinks.

Him: Fill me up!

Cat: I think it's time for an oil change, virgin olive oil, that is!
Van: Two of my favorite things—shopping AND eating!

Sushi Zen
41 Whitaker Street
912-233-1188

Located in the heart of the historic district, Sushi Zen offers something different for those who crave sushi. The restaurant is very small and cozy, with 8 seats at the sushi bar where you can watch the sushi chef work, and a few tables in the restaurant. There is also a balcony that offers the more traditional tables where you can sit on comfortable floor pillows in front of a low table.

With sushi, the appearance is just as important as the taste, and Sushi Zen does well with both. Nigiri Sushi is excellent, or if you prefer, the Philadelphia Roll, the Rainbow Roll, and the Spider Roll are particularly good. Our favorite is the Dancing Roll a combination of smoked eel, crab and avocado. There are several Asian beers available as well as sake, which is served hot or cold.

Dinners are also offered and the dishes can be served as grilled, tempura or cutlet, so if sushi is not a favorite, you can enjoy one of these dishes. Our non-sushi participant ordered the teriyaki chicken which came with Miso soup (seaweed, tofu, miso paste, and water) fried or white rice and a salad with ginger dressing.

You can finish off your meal with either the plum ice cream or green tea ice cream.

Van: It's a little known fact that it's bad luck to pour your own Sake.
Him: Is Sushi Zen related to Feng Shui?
Cat: YOU are so NOT Feng Shui!

Tapas
314 West Saint Julian Street
912-790-7175

Tapas, located in City Market, serves over 40 different dishes in an indoor-outdoor café-style seating.

For the uninitiated, the word "tapa" means "cover" in Spanish. Many years ago, bartenders would put a "cover" on top of drinks to keep gnats out of the drinks. Over time, the covers evolved into tiny plates, and with an empty plate on top of the glass, the establishments began placing small snacks on top of the plates. Thus, tapas bars were places one could go to drink and sample the many snacks that were offered by the inn.

The outside tables are fun and offer a view of the some-times craziness of City Market. If there is a chill in the air, the outdoor heaters can keep you cozy. In warm weather, the umbrellas protect you from the sun. The aluminum tables and chairs attest to the informal atmosphere of the restaurant. French bread served with olive oil, heavy herbs, and parmesan cheese is brought immediately as a starter.

Some of the dishes recommend include She Crab Soup with cayenne pepper, Sea Scallops with cream and garlic, Artichoke Ravioli, the Assortment of Sausage (including Andouille, Bratwurst, Buffalo, Boar, and Chorizo), Exotic Alligator Ribs, Crab Meat Rangoon, Reuben Egg Rolls, Spinach Terrine, Peppered Ostrich Steak, and Grilled Quail in Béarnaise sauce.

If you still have room for dessert, try the Chocolate Chip Bourbon Pecan Pie, Savannah Cream Cake, and Key Lime-Raspberry Cheesecake.

Tapas is an easy place to eat a lot or a little while you're roaming around City Market.

Him: I thought we were going to a 'topless' restaurant!
Van: I thought she said taps like in dancing!
Cat: This is absolutely the last time I will try to educate y'all about fine dining!

Vic's on the River

26 E. Bay Street or 15 East River Street
912-721-1000

Vic's is located in an antebellum refurbished four-story cotton warehouse with high ceilings and windows overlooking the Savannah River. It has become a well guarded secret to the food snobs in Savannah as it is an establishment of the highest caliber.

Prior to dinner, you might want to order a martini from their martini menu and listen to the piano player performing Johnny Mercer melodies. Sherman's troops used the warehouse as headquarters during the Yankee occupation of Savannah. In fact there is a map that was painted by Union troops directly onto the plaster to demonstrate their understanding of the territory between Tennessee, Georgia and South Carolina.

Vic's serves traditional Southern food as well as fresh seafood. For appetizers, we recommend the Jumbo Lump Crab Cake with remoulade sauce and three pepper relish, Fried Green Tomatoes with goat cheese and tomato chutney, Baked Oysters with asiago cheese, Pulled Pork Egg Roll with BBQ sauce and peach chutney, and Brie and Lump Crab Fondue with truffle oil and toast points.
Save some room for the excellent southern biscuits with apricot preserves.

For your main course, we can recommend Pan Seared Jumbo Scallops with jumbo lump crab risotto and wilted arugula, Wild Georgia Shrimp and Stone Ground Grits with andouille sausage and tasso ham gravy, Crab Stuffed Salmon with lemon grits and haricot vert, and Certified Black Angus Prime Rib with blue cheese butter, horseradish mashed potatoes, and grilled asparagus.

Our favorite dessert at all visits is the Bourbon Chocolate Pecan Pie … if you have room! After dinner you can take the elevator to the first floor and have coffee at Vic's Coffee Shop and then stroll along River Street.

Cat: Thank goodness that Sherman did not burn Savannah.
Van: Instead he gave the city to President Lincoln as a Christmas present.
Him: Wow, Santa never bought me a Christmas present like that!!

Window's Restaurant

2 West Bay Street
912-238-1234

Windows is located in the newly renovated Hyatt Regency Hotel, and it has truly captured the romantic essence of Savannah. The views are exquisite; you feel that you are right on the river, being carried upstream by one of the large container ship.

To enjoy your river ambience, start with the Ahi Tuna served with seaweed salad and cucumber slaw. The Steamed Mussels with roasted garlic, sherry and herbs, along with Crispy Calamari with chili pepper aioli are also a must.

The menu is simple at Windows, which is usually indicative of excellence, and it is very true in this case. Steaks are cooked over an open flame, producing mouth watering char flavor, number 1 favorite is the Chicago Style Bone-in Ribeye Steak. A special is the Lobster Mac and Cheese, that's right—our childhood favorite all grown up with the addition of lobster! There is also Shrimp and Grits, Crabmeat Fettuccine, Swordfish with Boursin cheese and the local catch of the day.

There are many restaurants around the world that are called Windows, but we do not believe that there are many that can show the river life and huge ships as "up close and personal" as the Windows Restaurant in Savannah. Combined with the excellence of the cuisine, it truly gives you vision!

Him: I don't even need my glasses!
Cat: Look at all those sailors!
Van: This is a favorite port for everyone: pretty girls, great drinks, and the "to-go cup!"

Savannah Originals Not to be Missed—Located Outside the Historic Area

Elizabeth's on 37th

107 East 37th Street
912-236-5547

To eat is just mundane, but to dine, that is sublime! And 'dine' is what you will do at Elizabeth's on 37th. This is probably one of the most famous restaurants of Savannah, having won accolades from everyone in the epicurean arena, including James Beard, Forbes Top 40 Restaurants in America, Wine Spectator, and Food & Wine Magazine. The restaurant was created by Elizabeth Terry and her husband Michael, who incorporated a vast knowledge of wine and southern food with the 20th and 21st century.

The menu changes daily, and is decided upon according to the fresh ingredients located at the market, and also the large herb and vegetable garden located at the restaurant.

Elizabeth's is known for the "taste treats"—small bites that can only serve to whet your appetite and experience taste bud Nirvana. The wines are carefully chosen and will not only complement but will enhance your meal. Oysters, roasted different ways: in herb butter; with champagne and caviar; with country ham, green onions, pernod, served over brioche; Stuffed Vidalia onions, and Black-eyed Pea Cakes with greens and curry cream are but a few examples of local culinary delights!

A delicious Dinner Salad comes with field greens, including mint, goat cheese, marinated peas and Elizabeth's own vinaigrette. We can vouch for Spicy Savannah Red Rice with Georgia Shrimp and clams, sausage and okra, Broiled Mustard-Garlic Glazed Salmon (with steamed collards in raspberry vinaigrette and rosemary new potatoes), Dry Rub Pork Tenderloin, Roast Quail with mustard-pepper sauce and apricot-pecan chutney and the Pepper Crusted Beef Tenderloin with Madeira sauce and scalloped potatoes.

The homemade desserts that are big hits included the Savannah Cream Cake, Triple Chocolate Torte, and Almond Pie. The mansion is elegant, the atmosphere is romantic, and the food is divine. This truly is the 'diva' of Savannah!

Him: I visit there often, so often in fact, that I call her Liz.
Van: Oh, yeah, you're the height of elegance.
Cat: Children, let's just get along and enjoy the dinner.

Johnny Harris

1651 East Victory Drive
912-354-7810

The Johnny Harris Restaurant bills itself as, "Savannah's Oldest and Most Popular Restaurant" and it is not wrong! Known for its barbecue, Johnny Harris has been in operation since 1924. It was tradition for many a Savannah family to dine there every Saturday evening and dance "under the stars" which are stars in the rounded ceiling of the dining room. Murals are painted on the walls, which contributes to the feeling of dining "al fresco." In addition to the "ballroom" restaurant, there is also The Kitchen where there is a quick luncheon bar and take-out available as well as a bar area with additional tables. Other unique characteristics stand out. At each private booth there is a doorbell-type "Service Bell," which, when rung, will bring the waitress to your table.

For appetizers, we recommend the Onion Blossom (with spicy Firecracker sauce), Fried Asparagus (with horseradish sauce), Barbecue Boats (potato skins stuffed with smoked pork and topped with barbecue sauce, melted cheese and sour cream), Crab and Spinach Dip, and Brunswick Stew (an original recipe with chicken, pork, beef and vegetables).

Suggested entrees include the Filet Mignon (Angus beef), Signature Prime Rib, Famous Half-fried Chicken, Crabmeat Au Gratin, Atlantic Salmon, and Barbeque Pork Plate (hickory and oak smoked, hand pulled from Boston Butts). Meals are served with several side dish choices and a Bread Basket with seasoned butter and garlic cheese spread. Additionally, we were told by one patron that as long as the ingredients are in the kitchen, they will prepare anything you request. For example, an omelet is not on the menu, but if you ask for one, they will fix it for you.

For a trip down Memory Lane, we highly recommend Johnny Harris. Relax, enjoy, and look at the stars!

Him: Can we sing "Moon River?"
Van: Puh-lease! This is about "Twinkle, Twinkle, Little Star."
Cat: The food here is the STAR!

Which Way to Tybee?

Crab Shack

40 Estill Hammock Rd
Tybee Island
912-786-9857

If you enjoy crab, you can't find a better place for sampling it then at the Crab Shack on Tybee Island. One can sit on the spacious outdoor deck overlooking the water or in the screened-in dining room as fans keep you cool in summer and heaters keep you warm in cold weather. The Gator Deck and Gator Shack provide safe interaction with the one year old alligators that can be fed treats by adults and children.

This is definitely the place to indulge in steamed or boiled seafood, a healthy alternative to the fried seafood offered at other Island restaurants. For appetizers, try some of the Oysters, Crabs or Crawfish. Great entrees include Alaskan King Crab (the biggest, best, sweetest crab you can find), local Blue Crabs, Dungeness Crabs, Stone Crabs, Snow Crabs, Deviled Crab, and Crab Cakes (AKA the Bubba Gump of crab!!!!) They also serve up a wonderful Low Country Boil, a stew of shrimp, corn, potatoes and sausage. If you can't make up your mind, try the Capt'n Crab's Sampler, a huge platter piled high with an assortment of shellfish in season including boiled shrimp, crawfish, Dungeness crabs, blue crabs, clams and mussels.

This is a time to roll up your sleeves and dig in. You can make a mess at your table as you crack the crab legs, and then just dump your shells and crumbs in the hole in the middle of the table. The desserts, Key Lime Pie and Turtle Cheesecake are small portions, but they add a sweet taste to the end of the meal.

Sitting dockside, seeing the dolphins, watching the sunset and sipping a beer? It just doesn't get any better than this!

Cat: Please pass me the paper towels!
Van: Do they give discounts for crabby people?
Him: Hey, I think I just saw Flipper!!

Hunter House

1701 Butler Avenue
Tybee Island
912-786-7515

Hunter House was built in 1910 as a family beach house and was refurbished in the 1990s to be a restaurant and bed and breakfast with four guest rooms. One has to walk up the steps to the second floor entrance which is off the Victorian verandah. Normally, the owner, John Hunter, is there to greet you, adding a very personal touch.

As in most coastal restaurants, seafood dominates the menu! Different specials are prepared each night, according to what is local and what is fresh. To start, Seafood Bisque laced with cognac includes shrimp, lobster and lump crab meat, Cuban Black Bean Soup is topped with a spicy sofrito salsa, and Crab Cakes with Cajun spices are served with tomato chutney.

Entrees include: Chilean Sea Bass topped with apple bark smoked-bacon and served over Boursin cheese-garlic-chive mashed potatoes; Black Grouper—Roasted (served with macadamia nut pesto),—Broiled (with roasted red pepper saffron aioli), or—Grilled (with a spicy Caribbean jerk marinade and Cuban black beans); and Ahi Tuna seared with a bourbon soy glace with jasmine rice.

For the landlubber, we highly recommend the Pot Roast Dinner which is served with mashed potatoes, gravy, green beans, buttered carrots, and tangy red cabbage, even better than Grandma used to make. The Filet Mignon is also a delicious choice with sautéed mushrooms, cognac glace, served with a three cheese topped twice baked potato and julienne vegetables.

Don't forget to take advantage of the verandah, either before your meal or after. You can enjoy the soft breezes as the restaurant is several blocks from the ocean.

Him: I don't get this verandah. It's a porch!
Van: Where is Rhett when I need him?
Cat: Whatever you call it, I love sitting in the rocking chair.

The Breakfast Club

1500 Butler Avenue
Tybee Island
912-786-5984

The Breakfast Club is an entity of its own and, thank the good Lord, it is located at Tybee Island, Ga.! Just look for the long line on 16th Street, and you will know that you are there! However, do not let the line daunt you as it moves quickly, and you will meet many nice people, maybe even a movie star or two! (Sandra Bullock, Ben Affleck).

Jody Sandowski, the owner of the Breakfast Club, is a graduate of the Culinary Institute of America and his expertise shows in the "rise and shine" of morning cuisine. To sit at the counter and observe the line cooks is like watching the Chicago Bears execute an intricate play during the Super Bowl! (Jody is from Chicago, and his menu is very reflective of his hometown).

Jody only cooks with fresh, local ingredients, "Davis Tomatoes" included. There are always specials, fish and grits, pork chops, steak and eggs of any style. A favorite is Helen's Solidarity (or Grill Cleaners Special) which is an omelette with onions, green peppers, potatoes, sausage—you get the message.... Anything on the grill goes....!

The menu has any breakfast food available, from fast order to gourmet delicacies. However, the Chicago Bear Burger deserves special mention. This is a hamburger that Wimpie would die for.... the one that the juice rolls down your arms ... the one with the homemade bun ... the one that all other hamburgers are "wanna be's"! Order it with everything, and we guarantee that it will be <u>the</u> burger that makes all hamburgers pale in comparison.

As a side note, Jody was the chef at John Kennedy Jr.'s wedding on Cumberland Island. Need we say more as to the quality and expertise of this incredible chef? It's not a "good morning" unless it's a Breakfast Club Morning

Cat: This is the most popular club in town!
Him: Do they serve a Falcon Burger?
Van: Since this is a club, maybe "Him" can be excluded from the membership!

Uncle Bubba's

104 Bryan Woods Road
Tybee Island
912-897-6101

On the road to Tybee Island, stop at Uncle Bubba's Oyster House for some down home cookin'. Uncle Bubba, best known as Paula Deen's brother, is the "sister" restaurant of The Lady and Sons, and both share some of the same specialties. Uncle Bubba's has outstanding views of Turner's Creek from the indoor dining room and the outdoor deck. A highlight of the restaurant is the oyster pit on the dining room floor where guests can see the oyster shuckers shucking, and smell the oysters being grilled.

The specialty of the house is of course, oysters served raw or steamed. Other appetizers include Shore is Good Seafood Dip (which Bubba stole "from the Lady and Sons cause it's the best!"), Crab Stew ("If you liked it at The Lady and Sons, you'll love it here"), and Deviled Crab ("our old family recipe").

While Lady and Sons specializes in Southern cooking, Uncle Bubba specializes in seafood, mostly fried. Po Bubba's (Uncle Bubba's version of Po'Boys) and Baskets include fried oysters, shrimp, crab cake, scallops, grouper, or chicken. Each day there is a blue plate special called Paula's Plate that comes with meat and two sides. The Seafood Pot Pie and Shrimp and Grits were delicious and more than ample for one person. The Low Country Boil, a specialty of the area, includes Wild Georgia shrimp, smoked sausage, corn on the cob and new potatoes.

We enjoyed the Pecan Pie with Vanilla Bean ice cream and Strawberry Shortcake made from Grandma Paul's Sour cream pound cake. There is even a special menu for Little Bubbas.

Him: Most anyone who lives in the south has an Uncle Bubba.
Van: But ... no Uncle Bubba can cook like this Uncle Bubba!
Cat: Yikes! Does anybody broil seafood anywhere?

Savannah's Bar Food

AJ's Dockside Restaurant
*1315 Chatham Ave
Tybee Island
912-786-9533*

AJ's offers waterfront dining and the best sunset view offered in the area. Add Flipper (dolphins) swimming by as you eat and it becomes a magical experience.

For appetizers, we suggest Hot Artichokes and Spinach Dip, Blackened Shrimp and Grits, and of course you can never go wrong with the pound of Boiled Shrimp. Sandwiches are simple: Burgers, Crawfish Cake Sandwich and Po Boys. The entrees we can recommend include Crispy Scored Grouper, Jambalaya Pasta, and any of their fried selections: Fried Oysters, Fried Scallops, Fried Shrimp, the Seafood Combo, and the Shrimp Burger.

The restaurant boasts 42 different types of beer, so you're sure to find something you like.

Cat: What a beautiful sunset!
Him: I think I'll sample all 42 brands of beer.
Van: A new movie: "Dancing with the Dolphins!"

B & D Burgers
*13 E. Broughton St.
912-231-0986*

If you're looking for the best burger in Savannah, you'll find it at B&D. The place is normally packed by noon, so go early. The burgers come in three sizes: 1/3 pound, ½ pound and one pound. You can order the ½ pound burger and still feel as if you've made the "lite" choice. After you've made your size selection, then you have to determine the type. Plain is great, but you might be interested in trying the Pulaski (burger topped with chili and cheddar-jack cheese), the Tomochichi (egg on it), the Moon River (with provolone and mushroom, or the BBB (blue cheese and bacon). You'll also find that the kitchen prepares your burger exactly as requested. You need to try the "Fry of the Week" which can vary from Cajun to cheddar cheese. Don't let the faux-Mexican atmosphere fool you! This place knows how to serve a burger.

Cat: I'll have the 'lite' burger.
Van: You do know that it is ½ pound of meat!
Him: Wimpy eats here!

Bernie's

115 E River St # 104
912-236-1827

The good news is the seafood is still great; however, the local musicians have been replaced by Karaoke. We think that still makes them "local" musicians. While the talent was disappointing, the seafood certainly wasn't. The dollar bills have been replaced by writing on the wall.

The Shrimp and Oysters (fried, raw, or steamed) can be a platter, basket or Po'Boy Sandwich. Try the Stuffed Shrimp, along with the Buffalo Shrimp. Who says that Buffalo is only for chicken wings?

The house specialty drink remains the Bernie's Mason Jar Bloody Mary. You can even buy the mix to go. Great bar! Great food!

Him: First place I've been to that has more graffiti in the dining room than in the bathroom!
Van: I always knew your mind was in the gutter!
Cat: Maybe if I collect enough Mason Jar Bloody Marys, I will "can" him!

Bonna Bella Yacht Club
2470 Livingston Ave
912-352-3133

We're going to tell you a secret, but please keep it a secret: Bonna Bella Yacht Club. There are few places in Savannah that one can reach by boat or by car, so follow us to Bonna Bella's. By car, go to the end of Derenne (and then right on Laroche and left on Livingston). By boat, take the Wilmington to the Herb River. We arrived once by boat and once by car; but each time we left by taxi.

Cat's prayers have been answered as the seafood is not fried, but grilled, steamed or blackened. The catch of the day is so fresh, you'd swear you caught it yourself on the dock of the restaurant.

This place is an old marina converted to a tiki-bar restaurant. The Shrimp Taco is accompanied by black beans and rice and a touch of Iavanozzi's special salsa. Now, let's get down to serious business. What should we have? Mac's Margarita or a Corona?

Cat: Travis Megee's in Cedar Key!
Van: "Wasting away again in Margaritaville!"
Him: So, do I turn right or left on the Herb River

Churchill's Restaurant & Tavern
13-17 W. Bay St.
912-232-8501

Churchill's Pub offers all the comforts and atmosphere of an authentic British pub, right in Savannah. When you open the door to the pub, you enter the bar area with a massive 34-foot hand-carved mahogany bar built in England. There is also a roof-top terrace for outdoor dining

Traditional English dishes include homemade Bangers and Mash (English sausage and mashed potatoes), Shepherd's Pie (ground beef, peas and carrots with a crust), Fish and Chips, Steak and Mushroom Pie, Lancashire Hot Pot (said to be like an Irish stew), and Bubble and Squeak (a casserole of ham, turkey, mashed potatoes and cabbage). The Ocean Pie, which is seafood with tomato and bacon, topped with mashed potatoes and browned gruyere cheese, is "absolutely scrumptious."

The Pub also carries 20 different draught beers (mostly European imports) and a large selection of American and European bottled beers as well as a full bar.

Him: Don't try the 20 draught beers from the roof terrace…
Van: I'm getting dizzy just thinking about it!
Cat: Cheers and tally-ho!

Creekside Grill

216 Johnny Mercer Blvd
912 898 4161

The Creekside Grill on Wilmington Island has a European outdoor café feel as well as a Key West feel to it. The outdoor landscaping around the creek out back makes it seem as if you are vacation.

If you're on a budget pretend-vacation, you can select the Baja Tacos and Crabcake Sandwich. On the other hand, the Filet Mignon and Crispy Scored Flounder are recommended for an upscale pretend-vacation. The menu has a wide variety of seafood, steak, salads and a great wine list.

Him: Do you think you can put a small boat in that creek?
Van: I think you could put your toy boat from your bathtub in the creek.
Cat: Have you noticed that he thinks everything "feels" like the Keys?

Creole Red
11 W. Bay
912-234-6690

Now strategically located on Bay Street, the decor of Creole Red's really does capture the feel of the Big Easy. Once seated, we liked how Creole Red himself greeted every customer at their tables.

We can recommend Crawfish Etoufee, Shrimp Creole, Jambalaya, Red Beans and Rice, and Oyster Po'boy. Although this is billed as the only Creole restaurant in Savannah, we think that the restaurant caters to the "light spicy" tourist crowd, as we found most of the dishes lacking in "heat." They can "bump it up a notch" for spiciness. They do have an in-house bar and feature live music on the weekends. The bar selection is excellent

Him: Did you see how Creole Red knew me when we came in?
Cat: You idiot! He greets everyone.
Van: His brain cells are burned by too much Tabasco!

Crystal Beer Parlor
301 West Jones Street
912-443-9200

The best place to get a hamburger in Savannah is a tie between B&D and Crystal Beer Parlor. According to Shirley, an employee since 1973, the menu has hasn't changed since 1933. The rich red wood everywhere and the pictures of Old Savannah puts this spot as the top contestant in the atmosphere category. There are pictures for former servers that include Johnny Mercer and even John Rousakis (long time mayor of Savannah, R.I.P).

The classic Corn Bread and Crab Soup are delicious, but you also have to have a hamburger and either onion rings or fries. It doesn't matter if you are a local who feels nostalgic or a history buff with an appetite, this is a must when dining in Savannah.

Van: Why didn't you tell me about the homemade potato chips?

Cat: And the signature Chili Cheese Jumbo Hot Dogs?
Him: And the fact that it is known as the last Savannah speakeasy?

Jen's and Friends
7 E Congress Street
912-238-5367

It's hard to believe a small cubby hole off Johnson Square could make this into a pretty cool bar. The bar is six foot nothing and a hundred pounds soaking wet, yet it shows a lot of spunk. The bar area is accented with a champagne glass chandelier, even though the menu is covered with naked dancing olives.

There are sandwiches and a salad bar which just may be the best salad bar in the downtown area. The sandwiches are served with chips, which you can replace with a trip to the salad bar. Local musicians play here and the sidewalk is used to accommodate the overflow.

Him: Is it just my imagination or is there a naked olive dancing on my menu?
Van: You see "naked" on that menu?
Cat: Just get your mind out of the olive jar!

Kevin Barry's Irish Pub
117 W. River Street
912-233-9626

Kevin Barry's is a great little Irish pub that features Irish folk music all week long. (For the history-minded, Kevin Barry was the first person executed during the War of Irish Independence.) There is no better place to be on St. Patrick's Day, but it is also a friendly place at other times. The place is easy to find, as there are displays of American and Irish flags outside. The upstairs bar has a generous display of military memorabilia as well as American flags.

Start your nibbling off with the K.B. Sampler that includes Cheese Sticks, Chicken Tenders, Jalapeno Poppers, and Mini Eggrolls which all help the beer go down faster. Sandwich offerings include All American Hamburger, Corned Beef on Rye, Ham & Cheese, Grilled Corned Beef and Grilled Reuben. Don't forget the great selection of Irish beers.

Him: Is Kevin Barry the owner?
Van: Faith and Begorrah—he died in 1920!
Cat: Erin Go Bragh!

Loco's Deli and Pub

301 W Broughton St
912-236-8711

Loco's roots are set in the Athens bar scene, and having much experience there, it's a very nice scene. Further rubbing it in that our college days are over, the patrons here are all kids. The college motif has a brazed Falcon flavor but the menu selection has a Southwestern flavor with a touch of wings. There is a variety of quesadillas on the menu as well as specialty sandwiches.

The night we visited there was a Trivia contest in process and the word around town is that the Texas Hold 'Em nights are fun too. Plasma televisions are the wallpaper of choice here, a major improvement from our college days.

Cat: Personally, I'm a Penn State fan. Is that what they call Georgia fans—Locos?
Van: "Georgia, hail to thee!"
Him: "And a hail to Georgia Tech."

Lulu's Chocolate Bar

42 Martin Luther King Blvd
912-238-2012

From the moment we walked in, we knew this place was a winner. From the juke box in the corner to out-of-this-world desserts, everything was top notch, including the prices. The selections on the juke box were as varied as the desserts on the menu. People were hanging out just to see which era the next song came from.

We sampled the Dreamsicle and Chocolate Mint from the dessert martini menu. We also tasted the Beerenauslese wine from the dessert wine menu. Other recommendations include the Raspberry Crème Brule and the Chocolate Covered Strawberries, as well as the Cayenne Pepper Truffles.

This is the place to go for desserts, even if it is a little pricey!

Van: The only true dessert destination in Savannah
Him: What about Krispy Kreme?
Cat: Oh, right, he's a real connoisseur!

McDonough's
21 E. McDonough Street
912-330-0925

McDonough's has been a mainstay in Chippewa Square, serving low priced drinks and great steaks for years. Recently McDonough's raised the bar and added an upstairs restaurant, "Billy's Place". The chef and staff is pretty much the old 45 South crew and if you are from Savannah, you know this is high praise indeed. At 10:00 PM the late night menu, with a lower pay scale becomes more of a bar food fare and originates from Billy's, the gourmet restaurant upstairs. In fact, Billy appears nightly talking to the patrons in a "Cheers" kind of way. Karaoke is very popular at McDonough's. The only thing more enjoyable than good karaoke is bad karaoke.

Him: A place where I know Billy's name.
Van: A lot of American Idol wanna-bes are there.
Cat: This place is like Cheers ... Where's Sam?

Mellow Mushroom

11 W Liberty St
912-495-0705

Mellow Mushroom is a Georgia-based restaurant that tends to follow the college crowd, with one in Athens at University of Georgia, one in Statesboro at Georgia Southern, and this one in Savannah, with SCAD (Savannah College of Art & Design) students. The place is known mostly for its pizza, and there is quite a variety of them. Try one of their classics such as White Pizza with garlic and sun dried tomatoes or one of the Pesto Pizzas. We also sampled the calzones and of course, the cold beer. They even have pitchers of Pabst Blue Ribbon. Its relaxing and eclectic atmosphere makes for a laid-back evening.

Him: I remember my mushrooms having a wilder taste in the seventies!
Van: Were the mushrooms magic or mellow?
Cat: Is that a thinly veiled seventies reference?

Molly MacPherson's Scottish Pub & Grill

311 W. Congress St.
912-239-9600

Molly MacPherson's is the only Scottish pub in Savannah and is known for their selection of Single Malt whiskeys. Be sure to check the huge world map to see if there is a pin from your town on the map where the question is asked, "Where are you from?"

Be sure to sample the Scottish fare that includes Cock-a-Leeky Soup, Scotch Broth, Scotch Eggs, and Potato Scones. The house special is Molly's Favorite (a turkey sandwich with sharp cheddar, green apple and maple butter). Other favorites are the Guinness Onion Rings, Guinness Pie, and Bangers & Mash.

If you're not familiar with single malts, this is the place to sample them. They offer flights (small tastings, similar to other places featuring beer or wine) of various single malts from different areas of Scotland.

Him: Why were all the waiters wearing skirts?

Van: Duh, those are kilts!
Cat: What do they really wear under those kilts?

Moon River Brewing Company
21 W. Bay Street
912-447-0943

Moon River Brewing Company is a restaurant, bar, and Savannah's only microbrewery. The giant brass vats proudly tell everyone that, if you want a fresh beer, sit down.

Appetizers we suggest are Moon River Crab Cakes with corn and black bean relish and roasted red bell pepper sauce, and Awesome Ossabaw Dip, a blend of cream cheese, roasted garlic, sun-dried tomatoes and scallions. There are a variety of sandwiches—we liked the Moon River Whammy and the Grilled Salmon Club—and salads and wraps.

Make sure to try one of their micro-beers, as they have interesting names, descriptions, and information about alcohol content, style, malts, bittering hops, and finishing hops. You can have a taster glass or a sampler.

Van: I think the hefenwiezen was the cloudy winner.
Cat: Why did they look at me when I ordered a Bud Lite?
Him: First documented case of drunk cow disease.

One-Eyed Lizzy's
417 East River Street
912-341-8897

One-Eyed Lizzy's has much to offer, the best being a balcony overlooking River Street and great margaritas. We could hear Buffett singing on the first two, but by number three, we could only hear a song that was a combination of Bob Marley and Jimi Hendrix. The food is definitely affordable and good to boot. We ordered the Burritos and the Tacos and they were "muy bien, gracias!" We think that is Mexican for "we are grateful to have authentic Tex-Mex here on River Street. Good service, good food, good prices. Now where are the mariachi singers?

Van: Pedro sez, "Chili today, hot tamale."
Cat: Pedro sez, "You never sausage a place."
Him: Pedro sez, "Juan Eye is great!"

Oyster Bar
411 E. River Street
912-232-1565

The Oyster Bar has been around for awhile and some consider it overdone, but not the loyal, local patrons! It has water chart wallpaper in the bathrooms and shellacked hatch covers, but to us that is nautical shabby chic! This place has a seafood feel to it, and sailors like to drink. The bar is the anchor of this ship, and it does have a friendly kind of feel. Anytime you take a well done atmosphere and soak it in rum, a good relaxing time is within grasp. We should also mention the food, right? If we were to recommend anything it would be the fresh catches.

Cat: He's been known to set anchor at a bar.
Van: He is the bar anchor.
Him: Anchor's Away, Captain!

Six Pence Pub
245 Bull Street
912-233-3151

The Six Pence Pub is a great neighborhood pub that won fame when featured as a backdrop in the movie, "Something to Talk About," when Julia Roberts confronts Dennis Quaid with another women. If the weather is favorable, try to get a table outside and watch the foot traffic go by.

There's not a better place in Savannah to have a Guinness and relax. This is a place to try the English dishes such as Pot Roast, Sheppard's Pie, Bangers and Mash, or just a sandwich (Turkey Club is great!). There is an impressive beer selection with English, Irish and Scottish brews on tap and bottled. Don't forget to check out the red telephone booth and the dartboards.

Him: I tried to make a call from the telephone booth.
Van: How much is six pences?
Cat: Well, the way the dollar is falling, who knows?

Spanky's
317 E. River Street
912-236-3009

Spanky's is one of River Street's oldest restaurants and taverns. It was voted Savannah's Best Bar Food and claims to be "Home of the Original Chicken Finger." There is always a crowd at Spanky's and you're sure to meet new friends there. The restaurant is open "all day," meaning it opens at 11 AM and closes at various late hours.

Spanky's has the best Chicken Fingers known to man, but we were disappointed that they no longer put horseradish in the honey sauce. Some things just should not be tampered with. This is as if McDonald's no longer put secret sauce on the Big Mac. We also ordered pizza, and as always, it is one of the better pizzas in town. The bar is usually loud—but that is what makes Spanky's fun.

Van: Spanky's reminds me of that place where everyone knows your name.
Him: Hey, I want you to meet my BFF, Alfalfa!
Cat: Is "The Gang" with him?

Tubby's Tank House

115 East River Street
912-233-0770

Tubby's is located in the heart of River Street and you can watch the container ships go by on the Savannah River while enjoying a cold one on the balcony. The drinks, however, are a little pricey, even by Savannah standards.

Start with Tubby's Chum, which we were somewhat reluctant to order, having fished with chum. We soon realized it was delicious crab stew. The Seafood Baskets were great as were the Buffalo Shrimp. Best of all were Tubby's Temptations including Pecan Pie, Key Lime Pie and the Cheesecake of the Day. They even have a Kids Menu consisting of Fried Shrimp, Chicken Nuggets, and Hot Dogs.

Cat: I need to walk off the tubbies after that meal!
Van: I'm falling in lubby with Tubby's!
Him: Old time traditions need old time prices.

Vinnie Van Go Go

317 Bryan Street
912-233-6394

Finding great pizza in the South is nearly impossible, but thanks to Vinnie Van Go Go's finding it has been made easy.

Vinnie's introduced authentic New York Pizza to Savannah and has been voted the #1 Pizza restaurant almost every year. The crust is light and crisp and all the toppings are fresh and flavorful. The menu has every pizza topping known to man, and also includes specialty pies. The beer selection is extensive and the focus is on specialty beers. Grab a seat in City Market, people watch, relax and enjoy. If you're tired from your day of shopping, touring or just partying, Vinnie's will deliver via pedal power, i.e. bicycle! Don't worry, it is guaranteed to be hot.

Vinnie's offers the character and quirkiness of real Savannah, along with great pizza—it's a combination that you do not want to miss!

Him: I need to buy the delivery boy a beer!
Van: Are you sure that pizza this good is in the South?
Cat: Are you sure we don't need reservations?

Wild Wing Café
27 Barnard St
912-790-9464

Wild Wing Café is continuing the tradition of its predecessor, Malone's, in showcasing local bands and setting the pace for City Market. Local talent, of course, does not mean Karaoke- wannabes, but actual local, performing bands. City Market attracts more locals than River Street, which is where the tourists seem to go. The best thing we can say about the chicken wings here is that there is something that separates them from the other wings which vary their wings by the degree of hotness. At Wild Wing's, the Thai wings taste different than Tao wings and Colorado Coppers are different from Jalapeno Cheddars. It's perfect bar food with a great outdoor setting.

Him: Do you think they have Buffalo Crab Cakes?
Van: Oh, that sounds really good.
Cat: He judges everything by the crab cakes.
Van: This is Wild Wings, not Wild Claws. Hey, that's our next book: a cookbook featuring Wild Buffalo Crab Claws! Do you think people will buy it?

Glossary of Savannah Food Terms

We in the South have always known that Southern cooking is as much of an art as French cooking. It is a combination of cuisines from Africa, France, Spain, England, Germany, the West Indies, as well as contributions from the Native American cuisine. In short, southern cooking is the "melting pot" of all cuisine. Again, like the French, we are passionate about our ingredients. Always fresh, we favor fat back, heavy cream, butter, pies, cakes, homemade pralines, and divinity ... definitely food for the soul. In order for y'all to understand the delectable dishes offered by our restaurants, we are providing a glossary of sorts to help you successfully eat your way through Savannah!

Barbeque: There are many different types of barbeque in the south, depending upon the region, and here in Savannah we tend to favor a tomato based sauce. North Carolina leans to a vinegar sauce, and South Carolina favors mustard based sauces. Personal tastes aside, the ritual of cooking the pork over an open pit or grill is akin to any other 'fine social' in the United States. Usually accompanied by a "toddy" or two, or three, or....

Boiled Peanuts: Many say that boiled peanuts are an acquired taste, but you'll just have to see for yourself. Raw peanuts are boiled in salt water until juicy and tender, and then eaten when hot. They are the southern equivalent to potato chips i.e. You just can't eat one!!!

Brunswick Stew: Originally dates back to the early 1800's and was made with squirrel. Today the main ingredients are beef, chicken, tomatoes, beans, okra, and corn. The Battle of the Brunswick stew still rages on between Brunswick, North Carolina; Brunswick, Georgia; and Brunswick County, Virginia. Of course, we all know that the best stew to be had is in Georgia ... Savannah that is!

Corn Bread: A true Southern specialty!! Cornbread should be crunchy on the outside, soft and moist on the inside. It is generally served as muffins or batter cakes at breakfast and as hoe cakes, Johnny cakes, corn dodgers, or fritters at dinner.

Dirty Rice: No, this is not rice that has fallen on the floor and according to the 3 second rule can be picked up and eaten!! It is rice that has a 'dirty' look due to the chopped or ground meat that has been added. It may also contain bacon, green peppers, and onions.

Frogmore Stew: See Low Country boil—both are the same, just from different areas.

Greens: There are a wide variety of greens; all are delicious, but very different in taste. Most are simmered with smoked ham hocks and spices, creating a delicious broth also known as pot likker. Greens are necessary on New Year's Day and bring good luck in the form of green money!

Grits: A staple on Southern tables, especially for breakfast. Grits are the small part of the corn kernel, and are wonderful when eaten with a butter bath and lots of salt and pepper.

Hominy: Very similar to grits, just larger in size. Here in Savannah, we all sing in "Hominy"!!!

Hoppin' John: A Southern tradition and a MUST for New Year's Day. It is a combination of black eyed peas, rice, and pork. Symbolizes good luck!

Hush Puppies: Corn meal dumplings that are deep fried and generally eaten as a side dish. Rumor has it that the name derived from the Civil War when the army cooks would fry the dumplings and throw them to the dogs to "hush them up".

Low Country Boil: A social tradition of the Low Country! Consists of shrimp, sausage, onions, potatoes, corn on the cob and a blend of seasonings, all cooked together. Some call it the Nectar of the Gods. Perfect for a large crowd, or just an excuse to gather, eat and drink beer!

Pilaus: AKA "perlews." A rice dish that has fried bacon, seasonings, meat, and vegetables.

Pralines: A candy that is as Southern as R.C. Cola and Moon pies. It is a mixture of boiled sugar and pecans—definitely not for the calorie counting individual.

Shad Roe: Rock fish eggs, great with scrambled eggs. We call it Bubba's caviar!

She-Crab Soup: A thick, cream based soup made from the delicious, sweet meat of the female crab. (This is not to be confused with He Crab Soup—a generally bitter, angry version of She Crab Soup!).

Shrimp Paste: Finely minced shrimp mixed with sweet butter, sherry, cayenne pepper, and other spices.... perfect on a cracker or mixed with hot grits.

Toddy: A cocktail, usually not consumed in the singular tense!!

Trifle: The best dessert ever invented! A layered concoction consisting of pound cake soaked in rum, layered with vanilla custard, strawberries, and whipped cream. It is often served in a large glass pedestal glass bowl, so the presentation is just as appealing as the taste!

Vidalia Onions: The best onions in the world! Very sweet, many eat them like apple! They can be served many ways i.e. casseroles, stuffed, baked, fried, you name it, we can do it!

Parking in Savannah

There are 3,000 parking meters in Savannah's Historic District with time limits ranging from 15 minutes to 10 hours. The cost per hour for parking on the meters ranges from $.30 per hour to $.75 per hour depending on the location of the meter. Parking meter rates in the three River Street parking lots is $1.00 per hour.

Parking meter, as well as time limit zone, regulations **are enforced Monday through Friday from 8AM until 5PM.** You do not have to feed the meters after 5 PM during the week and not at all on weekends. However, safety regulations, fire hydrants, fire lanes, yellow lines, etc., are enforced **24 hours a day, seven days a week** by Parking Services and the Savannah Police Department.

During the Ellis Square project, Robinson and State Street Parking Garages are **FREE on nights and weekends.** The garages are patrolled by security officers, and are conveniently located to various locations downtown.

City Garages:

- **Robinson Garage**—York and Montgomery Streets—912-651-6478
  Hours of operation: 24 hours a day/seven days a week

- **State Street Garage**—State and Abercorn Streets—912-651-6473
  Hours of Operation: Monday Through Friday 6AM until 1AM; Saturday 5AM until 3AM; Sunday 5AM until 1AM

- **Bryan Street Garage**—Bryan and Abercorn Streets—912-651-6477
  Hours of Operation: 24 hours a day/seven days a week

- **Liberty Street Garage**—Liberty and Montgomery Streets (912) 644-5934
  Hours of operation: Monday through Friday 6AM until 1AM; Saturday 5AM until 3AM; Sunday 5AM until 1AM

All Garages: Daily rates (hourly parking), $1 for the first hour and $.75 for each additional hour or portion thereof

978-0-595-48632-8
0-595-48632-0

Printed in the United States
129178LV00004B/304-390/P